Power

Key Concepts

POWER

John Scott

Polity

First published in 2001 by Polity Press in association with Blackwell
Publishers Ltd.

Editorial office:
Polity Press
65 Bridge Street
Cambridge CB2 1UR, UK

Marketing and production:
Blackwell Publishers Ltd
108 Cowley Road
Oxford OX4 1JF, UK

Published in the USA by
Blackwell Publishers Inc.
350 Main Street
Malden, MA 02148, USA

A catalogue record for this book is available from the British Library.

Library of Congress Cataloging-in-Publication Data

Scott, John, 1949–
  Power / John Scott.
    p.   cm. – (Key concepts)
  Includes bibliographical references and index.
    ISBN 0-7456-2417-0 (HB : acid-free paper) – ISBN 0-7456-2418-9
  (pbk. : acid-free paper)
    1. Power (Social sciences) I. Title. II. Series.
  HM1256 .S26 2001
  302.3 – dc21   2001001568

Typeset in 10.5 on 12 pt Sabon
by Best-set Typesetter Ltd., Hong Kong
Printed in Great Britain by TJ International, Padstow, Cornwall

This book is printed on acid-free paper.

Contents

Acknowledgements

Drafts of the general framework for this book have been presented and discussed at seminars at Essex University and Bergen University. Issues raised in various chapters have been discussed at a number of seminars and conferences over the years. I am grateful to colleagues and students for comments received on these ideas. I am particularly grateful to José López, who read and commented on a version of the first two chapters.

John Scott

1
Patterns of Power

In its most general sense, power is the production of causal effects. It is 'the bringing about of consequences' (Lukes 1978: 634; Lukes 1986). The power of a river, for example, is manifest in its causal effects: it erodes a bed, transports rock material from one place to another, and produces a delta or a flood plain. Similarly, the power of electricity is manifest in the illumination of light bulbs, the heating of cooker elements, and the operation of underground railways. This idea of power as *causal power* is also integral to the very idea of human agency: to be an agent is to exercise causal powers that produce specific effects in the world. These human powers comprise the 'transformative capacity' possessed by human agents (Giddens 1976: 110; Giddens 1982). To act is to have causal powers, and these powers constitute the 'potency' that defines an organism as a human agent. Power is 'an actor's general ability to produce successful performances' (Wrong 1979: 1).[1]

To talk or to write about *social* power involves a move beyond this basic causal vocabulary. Social power is a form of causation that has its effects in and through social relations (Isaac 1992; see also Isaac 1987). In its strongest sense, it is an agent's intentional use of causal powers to affect the conduct of other participants in the social relations that connect them together. In this book, my concern is with social power in this sense and, unless anything is stated to the contrary, the word 'power' will be used exclusively in its social sense.

At its simplest, power is a social relation between two agents, who may usefully be called the 'principal' and the 'subaltern'.[2] A principal is the paramount agent in a power relationship, while a subaltern is the subordinate agent. The principal has or exercises power, while the subaltern is affected by this power. Concretely, of course, such relations are rarely so one-sided as this implies. A principal in one relationship may be a subaltern in another, and subalterns often exercise countervailing power to that of their principal. Analytically, however, the dynamics of power relations can initially be understood in terms of this relatively simple relation of principal to subaltern.

The intentions or interests of principals have been central to many discussions of power. To qualify as a social power relation there must be more than simply a causal influence between agents. It is for this reason that Wrong (1979) holds that it is a form of causal influence that involves the production of intended effects. An exercise of power, he argues, typically involves an intentional intervention in a chain of causal effects. An accidental or incidental effect of an agent's actions cannot be regarded as an exercise of power unless it is a foreseen consequence of these actions (1979: 4). A power relation, then, involves the intention to produce a particular effect or the desire to see a particular effect occurring. Power is an intended or desired causal effect; it is an effect that realises a purpose (Beetham 1991: 43). A power relation cannot, therefore, be identified unless there is some reference to the intentions and interests of the actors involved and, especially, to those of the principal (Wartenberg 1990: 65). An intention or a desire rests upon a felt or perceived interest that the principal believes will be furthered if he or she brings about particular kinds of causal effects in the field of social relations.

As agents, both principals and subalterns are, in crucial respects, free: they have a degree of autonomy in shaping their actions, which are never completely determined by external factors. This is not to say that individuals must be seen, in classical liberal terms, as sovereign individuals making perfectly informed and unconstrained rational choices on the basis of their pure 'free will'. It is, rather, to recognise that agents always have the ability to *choose* among alternative courses of action, however constrained these choices may be. Lukes (1974) has stressed that the most important implication of this is that social power has to be seen in relation to the possible resistance that others can offer to it. The subaltern must be thought of as being able to act otherwise than in conformity with the wishes of the principal, as having the capacity to resist. In Foucault's words, 'Power is exercised only over free subjects, and only in so far as they are free' (Foucault 1982: 229). The power of a principal consists in the ability to freely pursue intentions and interests; the power of a subaltern consists in their freedom to resist (Benton 1981: 296). Social power, in its most general sense, then, involves the socially significant affecting of one agent by another in the face of possible resistance.

The exercise of power and the possibility of resistance to it establish a dialectic of control and autonomy, a balance of power that limits the actions of the participants in their interplay with each other. In power relations, then, 'individual or collective subjects . . . are faced with a field of possibilities in which several ways of behaving, several reactions and diverse comportments may be realized' (Foucault 1982: 229). Acts of power occur when principals are able to restrict the choices that subalterns are able to make: the greater this restriction (the more limited the range of choices available to subalterns), the greater is the power of the principal (Wartenberg 1990: 85). As Lukes has put it:

> To use the vocabulary of power . . . is to speak of human agents separately or together, in groups or organisations, through action or inaction, significantly affecting the thoughts or actions of others. In speaking thus, one assumes that although agents operate within structurally determined limits, they none the less have a relative autonomy and could have acted differently.
> (Lukes 1977: 6–7)

Power relations involve the possibility of conflict because of this choice among alternatives, but resistance is not always expressed in overt conflict or struggle. Consider, for example, a factory manager who orders an employee, on the threat of dismissal, not to smoke at work. If the worker has no intention of smoking – and is, indeed, a non-smoker – then there will be no conflict and the manager has clearly not had to exercise any actual power to prevent the worker from smoking. The manager does, however, still hold the power of dismissal, which is ready and waiting to be exercised should this or any other worker choose to smoke at work. Power relations involve the possibility of conflict, but only the exercise of power need involve actual conflict, however minimal.

These considerations show how important it is to distinguish between *exercising* power and *holding* power (Dahl 1968). At its fullest, a power relation involves the deliberate, intentional intervention of a principal in the course of interaction so as to produce a specific and particular effect on a subaltern. Such an exercise of power comes closest to the everyday understanding of social power. An agent who has this capacity to affect others may, however, be able to achieve this without actually having to do anything at all. This occurs when others anticipate their intentions and their likely actions and act in relation to these. Such 'anticipated reactions' (Friedrich 1937) are apparent when agents act in a certain way because they believe that, if they do not, they will be affected in some socially significant way by another who has the capacity and the intention to do so.

Action on the basis of an anticipated reaction is an effect of a principal's power, even though he or she does nothing directly to make this power effective. Indeed, anticipated reactions may even increase a person's power. The leaders of a political party, for example, may believe that a business leader is wealthy enough to grant or withhold financial favours, and so may formulate policies that accord with his or her wishes. They may, however, misunderstand the true extent of the person's wealth, his or her actual financial power being amplified by the mistaken beliefs of the party leadership. Such reputational power should not be overstated, but neither should it be ignored:

If an actor is believed to be powerful, if he [*sic*] knows that others hold such a belief, and if he encourages it and resolves to make use of it by intervening in or punishing actions by the others who do not comply with his wishes, *then* he truly has power and his power has indeed been conferred on him by the attributions, perhaps initially without foundation, of others. (Wrong 1979: 9)

Power can be effected, then, without being exercised. This conclusion is central to the argument that power is, at root, a capacity. To have a capacity is to be in a position to do something (Morriss 1987: 81), and any capacity may remain latent without thereby ceasing to be a capacity. As Haugaard (1997) has succinctly put it, a Ferrari racing car has the power to travel at 120 miles per hour, even when it is parked in a garage with its engine switched off. Any disposition can persist without being exercised. Someone may, for example, know how to ride a bike even though they are not currently cycling. Their knowledge does not suddenly come into existence when they get on a bike and disappear again when they dismount. A principal may, therefore, have a capacity to act in some way without actually doing so. To have power is to have an enduring capacity or disposition to do something, regardless of whether this capacity is actually being exercised.

It could be suggested that an unexercised capacity might as well not exist, as it might not seem to make sense to describe someone as 'powerful' if they never do anything with their supposed power. However, a powerful person who does not exercise their power is like a miser who hoards a fortune but lives as a pauper. The miser retains the capacity to spend and could escape his or her poverty in an instant. Similarly, the actor with the potential to exercise power can, at any moment, choose to realise this potential by affecting the actions of others. Power – like knowledge and money – can be held in readiness for use whenever it is needed. The anticipation of its use, furthermore, means that power can have significant social consequences even when there is no explicit and overt intervention by the principal.

Mainstream and Second Stream

This core idea of power has been developed in two broad directions, forming two streams of power research (Ball 1975; Ball 1976; Clegg 1989). The mainstream tradition has been principally concerned with the episodically exercised power that one agent has over another. The second stream of power research focuses on the dispositional capacity to do something. It is the ability that actors have to facilitate certain things that lies at the centre of attention. Mainstream views concentrate on what in French is called '*pouvoir*', while the second stream has concentrated on '*puissance*'.[3]

The mainstream view of power takes the sovereign power of a state as its exemplar (Macpherson 1962; Abercrombie et al. 1986). The classic statement of this is in Weber's analysis of the structuring of authority and administration in modern and pre-modern states (Weber 1914). While later work on sovereign power has continued to focus on states and the political power of individuals and groups in relation to states, it has also followed Weber's recognition that power exists in other sovereign organisations, such as businesses and churches. Economic power, for example, has been studied in national and multinational enterprises and in the actions of the individuals and groups involved in their ownership and control, and in similar 'stakeholder' relations. A key area of research has been the relationship between economic power and political power, as explored in elitist and Marxist theories of ruling classes and power elites (Mosca 1896; Mills 1956; Miliband 1969).

Weber saw power as manifested in the chances that an actor's will can be imposed on the other participants in a social relationship, even against their resistance (Weber 1914: 942). According to this point of view, actors seek to make others do what they would otherwise not do, and they resist the attempts of others to make them act in ways contrary to their own preferences. In this 'constant sum' or 'zero sum' view, power relations are seen as asymmetrical, hierarchical relations of super- and sub-ordination in which one agent can gain only at the expense of another. They must be seen in terms of the conflicting interests and goals of the participants and the abilities of some to secure the compliance of others. There is a given distribution of power within any society, and some agents have more of this power than others. Struggles over the distribution of power will always involve both winners and losers.

This view of power was forged into a formal model by Lasswell and Kaplan (1950) and was given mathematical form by Simon (1953), Dahl (1957), and Polsby (1960). These writers, however, limited their attention to the behavioural and intentional aspects of the actual exercise of power. They saw power as the exercise of causal influence within the decision-making processes of sovereign organisations. Powerful actors are those who make decisions or who participate in the decision-making apparatuses of sovereign organisations. Dahl, for example, saw a principal having power over subalterns because he or she is able to make decisions to which subalterns conform.

This approach has largely been developed through a reliance on an individualistic and rationalistic view of action that stresses the autonomy and rationality of agents as they choose from among alternative courses of action. The paradigm example of such action is Weber's type of instrumentally rational action ('*zweckrationalität*'). In this framework, individuals have preferences, appetites, desires, or interests, and they pursue their own interests at the expense of those of others. Each agent is a maximiser, or satisficer, of advantages. Drawing on the rational-choice theories of market behaviour produced by economists, power relations in and around sovereign states have been investigated as if they formed a 'political market' (Downs 1957; Buchanan and Tullock 1962).

Thus, Dowding (1996) has argued that power should be seen as the capacity of one agent to deliberately change – in line with his or her own interests – the 'incentive structure' of costs and benefits faced by another agent. In a similar vein, Wartenberg (1990: 85) holds that an agent becomes a principal in a power relation if, and only if, that agent can strategically constrain the action alternatives available to a subaltern. The constrained alternatives form an integral element in the subaltern's strategic calculations about future courses of action, and their consideration of the rewards and costs attached to particular alternatives may lead subalterns to act contrary to certain of their own interests. What is important, Dowding argues, is that an altered incentive structure allows a principal to achieve desired outcomes by means of the actions of others.

This purely individualistic and rational-choice version of the mainstream view is more limited than Weber's own ideas on power, and this led writers such as Wrong (1967–8) and Bachrach and Baratz (1962; 1963) to emphasise a whole second face to the exercise of power. The first face of power, studied by Dahl and his followers, comprises the most obvious and overt processes of formal decision-making. The second face of power, on the other hand, comprises the hidden, behind-the-scenes processes of agenda setting that Bachrach and Baratz termed 'nondecision-making'. For Bachrach and Baratz, a principal has power over a subaltern to the extent that he or she can prevent the subaltern from doing something that they would otherwise do or that they would like to see happen. This can be achieved, for example, by preventing an issue from coming to the point of decision, thereby excluding the subaltern from any effective say about it.

Lukes's (1974) important critique of power studies was mainly concerned with the problems that he identified in this mainstream of power research. While he recognised the validity of distinguishing between the two facets of power – though he rather misleadingly described them as two 'dimensions' of power – he argued that it was also necessary to add a third facet to the analysis. This aspect of power took more seriously the importance of the 'real interests' of which actors may normally be unaware. From this point of view, Lukes argues, the power of a principal can be manifest in the ability to make a subaltern believe that their interest lies in doing something that is, in fact, harmful to them or contrary to their deeper interests.

This argument has generated much critical discussion about the nature of interests, but Lukes (1977) and some other contributors to this discussion (for example, Giddens 1982) have extended the argument to raise a matter that points beyond the bounds of the mainstream approach. In addition to the need to incorporate real interests and 'false consciousness' into the model of power, they pointed to the need to take social structure more seriously. Power is not limited to the 'discrete intervention by a social agent in the life of another social agent' (Wartenberg 1990: 72), but may also involve the existence of enduring structured constraints over actions. Lukes holds that this is most clearly apparent in what he calls the 'facilitative power' that may be held by classes and other collective actors. Though there are problems in Lukes's distinction between structural constraint and forms of structural determination that do not involve power (Layder 1985), he made the duality of structure and agency central to discussions of power.

In raising these issues, Lukes and Giddens were echoing ideas that had emerged as central themes in the second stream of power research. This second stream of research has not been so tightly defined as the mainstream, and it has no equivalent founding statement to that of Weber. It has, nevertheless, been an important source of critical commentary on that mainstream. The second stream begins from the same core idea of power, but it takes this in a different direction. Its focus is not on specific organisations of power, but on strategies and techniques of power. It sees power as diffused throughout a society, rather than being confined to sovereign organisations. According to this view, power is the collective property of whole systems of co-operating actors, of the fields of social relations within which particular actors are located. At the same time, it stresses not the repressive aspects of power but the facilitative or 'productive' aspects. Of particular importance are the communal mechanisms that result from the cultural, ideological, or discursive formations through which consensus is constituted. This is a 'variable sum' or 'nonzero sum' view of power: all can gain from the use of power, and there need be no losers.

A key figure in the development of this second stream is Gramsci (1926–37), whose concept of hegemony highlighted a mechanism of power through which a dominant class can secure the *consent* of subaltern classes without the need for any direct use of coercion or repression. Through the cultural formation of individuals in schools, churches, factories, and other agencies of socialisation, a dominant class can secure a more stable position for itself than it could possibly enjoy simply through exercising the repressive powers of a state. Althusser (1971) employed this idea, arguing that the 'repressive apparatuses' of a state work alongside its 'ideological apparatuses' to sustain social control. It is through ideology, he argued, that individuals are 'interpellated' – called out – as subjects with the specific characteristics and desires that commit them to the very actions that are required of them by their class position.

Working from a different theoretical basis, Arendt (1959) also stressed the collective capacities that are inherent in political communities. Power relations, she argued, are formed through communicative actions in discursive communities. People communicate with each other through their speech acts, and the shared symbols that they use allow them to co-ordinate their actions and so to act in concert. Power comes into existence wherever the members of a group are forged together through such bonds of solidarity and organise themselves for collective action. Such a group acquires an identity and purpose and enables or 'empowers' its constituent individuals to act in the name of, or on behalf of, the community as a whole (see also Lindblom 1977).

Habermas (1981a; 1981b) shares this view and adds that it is the discursive structures of the socio-cultural life-world that are the bases of such power. Habermas draws on the ideas of Parsons (1963), as well as Arendt, as it was Parsons who saw power as resting on a framework of communal trust and shared values within a 'societal community'.[4] According to Parsons, power is rooted in the shared values that define the goals and purposes of a community. Societal communities are seen as organised around those values in which individuals have trust or confidence, and that define positions of leadership whose occupants are endowed with the legitimate right to issue commands and to make policy in relation to the values and purposes that the members of the community hold in common. Parsons further argues that the diffused character of power makes it a circulating medium analogous to money. It is not confined to sovereign organisations but is something that all individuals can hold, in varying degrees, and can use or exchange in their actions.

Parsons has been criticised for overemphasising value consensus and for implying that societies are generally characterised by the perfect socialisation of their members into this consensus (Wrong 1961). In order to avoid this tendency in Parsons' work, Barnes (1988) has proposed an approach to power that opens up this argument and takes it in a more acceptable direction. For Barnes, the basis of social order is to be found in shared cognitive meanings – not shared values – and power, therefore, has to be related to the symbolic orders of meaning that underpin particular bodies of knowledge. Power is, he argues, a capacity for action that someone has by virtue of the social distribution of knowledge: an individual's power is their portion of the collective power of the community as a whole, the community whose knowledge they bear and share (1988: 57). It is particularly closely associated, he argues, with those communal structures of meaning that Weber saw as associated with social status and the social estimation of honour (1988: 144).

The most influential statement of this second-stream view of power in recent years has been that of Foucault (1975; 1976), who argued that analysis of the repressive powers of command within states and other sovereign organisations provides only a part of the full picture.[5] Power exists throughout the social sphere that surrounds and penetrates the public, political sphere of sovereign power. What Foucault called 'discursive formations' operate through mechanisms of socialisation and 'seduction' – to use a term from Baudrillard (1981) – that bring about the cultural formation of individual subjects. They bring particular kinds of mental orientation and routinised actions into being. Where Arendt and Parsons saw discursively formed power in a positive way, as a form of collective empowerment, Foucault stressed its negative face. For Foucault, it remains a source of social control, of 'discipline'. Discourse constitutes people as subjects who are authorised (as experts) to discipline others, but the most effective and pervasive forms of power occur where people learn to exercise self-discipline. Foucault studied, in particular, the asylums, prisons, schools, armies, and factories that helped to establish disciplined populations.

Foucault's argument, of course, owes much to both Gramsci and Althusser, though he stressed that power was not to be seen as the monolithic possession of a class or any other social agency. Disciplinary power is dispersed through all the groups, organisations, and agencies of a society, and there is no master plan of indoctrination at work. Societies tend to be highly fragmented, forming dispersed 'archipelagos' of localised discursive communities, each of which is the basis of its own specialised forms of power. Power is pluralistic and circulates through the whole society, though there may be certain common principles of power running through large parts of a society.

Lukes, Giddens, and others have sought to incorporate elements of this second stream into the mainstream. This does not mean – as is sometimes suggested – that the mainstream view must be completely replaced with, say, a Foucauldian view of power. The arguments of Foucault and others from within the second stream also have their flaws. The central task for research into power is to build an account that synthesises the two streams, using each to enrich the other. This is not to say that they are equally valid in all respects, nor is it to suggest that our aim should simply be an eclectic bolting together of disparate ideas. Rather, it is to claim that a work of synthesis that draws, in varying ways, on the two streams is a fundamental priority.

The Elementary Forms of Social Power

Mainstream and second-stream approaches have each highlighted different aspects of the core idea of power. Using ideas from these two streams of research, it is possible to distinguish two complementary modes of power. Mainstream research has highlighted what can be called corrective causal influences, while second-stream research has emphasised persuasive causal influence. Corrective influence and persuasive influence are the elementary forms of social power. While each depends on the use of resources, the type of resource and the ways in which they are used differ. The resources that are involved in these forms of influence are those that can be put to use as sanctions or that can be offered as reasons for acting. Concrete patterns of power combine corrective and persuasive influence in various ways, forming both stable and enduring structures of domination and more fluid structures of interpersonal power.

Corrective influence operates through the use of resources that can serve as punitive and remunerative sanctions that are able to work directly on the interests of subalterns in power relations. At their simplest, these resources may be tied to the physical strength and immediate physical possessions that a person can use in face-to-face encounters, but social power arises from the ways that they are socially structured and involves a more extended range of rewarding and punishing resources. The two sub-types of corrective influence are force and manipulation. Force is the use of negative physical sanctions to prevent the actions of subalterns, the key resources being weapons, prisons, and similar instruments. Manipulation, on the other hand, is a use of both positive and negative sanctions of various kinds, including such things as money, credit, and access to employment, in order to influence the interest-oriented calculations of agents. It is through force and manipulation that subalterns can be caused to act or be prevented from acting by direct restraint or by influence over the conditions under which they make their calculations.

Persuasive influence, on the other hand, operates through the offering and acceptance of reasons for acting in one way rather than another. At its simplest, this may rest upon a person's strength of personality and their attractiveness to others, but persuasiveness depends particularly on socially structured cognitive and evaluative symbols. Shared cognitive meanings and shared value commitments are bases on which intrinsically appropriate reasons for action can be offered to others and be regarded as plausible by them. A particular course of action comes to be seen as morally or emotionally appropriate. These resources are those that Bourdieu (1979) has called 'cultural' and 'symbolic capital'.

Force is the most basic and direct way that one agent has of altering the action alternatives open to another. It involves imposing physical restrictions or emotional suffering on another person. As such, it relies on the physical abilities of principals or on their ability to mobilise physical effects. Examples of force include inflicting pain or death, denying food, destroying property, and giving insults or abuse. In a force relationship, a principal physically or emotionally restrains a subaltern from pursuing a course of action that he or she would prefer to pursue, or behaves in a way that the subaltern would avoid if at all possible (Wrong 1979: 24–8; Wartenberg 1990: 93). Force can take both violent and non-violent forms. While violence consists of a direct force exercised on the body or mind of another person, non-violent force involves placing physical restraints on their freedom of action. The ability to make another's nose bleed by punching them in the face, for example, is an exercise of raw violence that significantly affects the other. Such an exercise of force, however, is at the limits of social power, as the subaltern has no choice of action. It is not possible for the subaltern to choose whether or not to have a nosebleed; it is an automatic physiological response to a hard punch on the nose. Force is a particularly negative or restrictive form of power that prevents a subaltern from doing something. It cannot so easily be used in positive ways to make a subaltern act in one way rather than another. This negative character of sheer force means that it tends to be experienced by subalterns in an alienating way and is especially likely to arouse feelings of hostility and acts of resistance.

What I have called manipulation occurs where a principal alters the bases on which a subaltern calculates among action alternatives, ensuring that the subaltern's rational choices lead him or her to act in ways that the principal desires. The intentions of the principal are hidden from the subaltern, yet the subaltern acts on the basis of conditions that have been set by the principal (Wrong 1979: 28–32). Examples of manipulation include advertising, propaganda, and price adjustment, where information, ideas, or prices are adjusted in order to secure particular outcomes. What is commonly described as 'brainwashing' can be seen as a mixture of manipulation and emotional force.[6]

Where corrective influence depends on rational calculation, persuasive influence depends on arguments, appeals, and reasons that cause subalterns to believe that it is appropriate to act in one way rather than another.[7] In this form of power subalterns are convinced of the need to follow a particular course of action through the building of emotional commitments that limit their willingness to consider action alternatives in a purely instrumental way. This may involve a commitment to or recognition of ideas or values that are accepted as beyond question, as providing intrinsically appropriate reasons for acting. Where persuasion operates through cognitive symbols – ideas and representations that lead people to define situations in certain ways – it takes the form of signification. Where it operates through the building of value commitments to particular ideas or conditions, it takes the form of legitimation (Giddens 1984: 29). In the former case, subalterns are drawn into a principal's interpretative frame of reference, while in the latter case they accord a normative character to the views of their principals. Those who are committed to a particular set of values are likely to defer to the views of those whom they regard as especially fitted to speak on behalf of these values, and so subalterns may build up a commitment to these agents themselves. Persuasive influence may also involve a commitment to those agents whose views are treated as especially compelling because of their particular character or competence. Trust in the superior medical knowledge of doctors, for example, is likely to lead their patients to accept diagnosis and advice. In yet other situations, persuasive influence may rest on an emotional attraction to a particular individual and may be sustained by rhetoric and demagoguery that reinforces this attraction.

Force, manipulation, signification, and legitimation are elementary forms of power. They are the elements from which more fully developed power relations may be built. They are not, in themselves, persistent and enduring relations of power, and they often lack some of the features of the more developed forms. In situations of force, for example, there are no real alternatives open to subalterns: options are physically blocked or prevented by the principal. In situations of manipulation, on the other hand, knowledge or awareness of the intentions of the principals is missing. In this case, and in some situations of persuasive influence, anticipatory reaction is not possible. Fully developed power relations, then, go beyond these elementary forms to include, to varying degrees, intentionality, resistance, and anticipated reactions.

Elementary forms of power	Corrective influence		Persuasive influence	
	Force	Manipulation	Signification	Legitimation
Developed forms of power	Domination			
	Through constraint		Through discursive formation	
	Coercion ('lions')	Inducement ('foxes')	Expertise ('owls')	Command ('bears')
	Counteraction			
	Protest		Pressure	
	Interpersonal power			

Figure 1 A map of power relations

Developed power relations, whether based in corrective influence or persuasive influence (or – as is more usual – on some combination of the two), can be seen at a number of levels. There are, first, those patterns of power that form structures of *domination*. Secondly, there are patterns of power that occur as forms of *counteraction* to domination. In addition to domination and counteraction, however, it is possible to distinguish the more amorphous but enduring patterns of *interpersonal power* that have their roots in proximal, face-to-face locales. These and related distinctions are set out in Figure 1.

Structures of Domination

Domination exists where power is structured into the stable and enduring social relations that make up large-scale social structures. It is 'canalised' power (Mannheim 1947: 48–9), working through institutions to produce regular and persistent patterns of action. Weber explored some aspects of domination in his investigations into patterns of social stratification. I shall not look in any detail at what he said on this as I have examined it in an earlier book where it was the central topic (Scott 1996). My interest here is with domination as the basis of *leadership* rather than social stratification. It is through leadership that some agents are constituted as principals with enduring powers over particular subalterns. While stratification and leadership cannot – and should not – be separated, the distinction is important to keep in mind.

Leadership within structures of domination occurs through specific extensions to the elementary forms of power that have been discussed. In most concrete structures of domination, of course, these forms of power will operate in combination, and they generally depend upon each other in complex ways. It is important, nevertheless, to understand their specific and distinctive features if we are to understand their concrete combinations.[8]

Force and manipulation, based on instrumentally rational or calculative forms of motivation and the use of material resources, can be organised into more complex structures of coercion and inducement (Giddens 1981: 57). These embed force and manipulation into larger and more complex alignments of interest through the threat of force and the promise of rewards. Together, coercion and inducement comprise what Weber (1914) described as structures of 'domination by virtue of a constellation of interests', and that Giddens (1979: 100–1) has called 'allocative domination'. They are structures of constraint, where principals can influence subalterns without using formal orders or directions. Subaltern action alternatives are shaped by the constellation of interests set by a principal's resources.

Persuasive influence, on the other hand, involves processes of legitimation and signification that can be organised into complex structures of command and expertise. These embed persuasive influence into larger and more complex structures of commitment, loyalty, and trust, using means of information and communication. They comprise what Weber called structures of 'domination by virtue of authority' and Giddens has called 'authoritative domination'. They are structures of discursive formation.

It is difficult to sustain a structure based on pure force for very long, as it requires the constant use of physical energy and resources. The establishment of a structure of leadership through coercion, however, allows a more economical use of these facilities, as it rests on a *threat* of force and on a belief on the part of the subalterns that the principal has both the capability and the willingness to use it. Coercion was seen by Machiavelli (1513) and Pareto (1916) as characteristic of those they called the 'lions' of political life – those who maintain their hold on power through repressive measures. A threat to use force alters the action alternatives open to a person by changing the reward and cost outcomes that are associated with particular courses of action. At its most extreme, coercion involves a threat to use violence, as in the case where a subaltern chooses to act as directed in order to avoid a punch in the face or a bullet in the head.[9] Submission to threatened violence is at the margins of social power.

Coercion need not involve the constant use of actual force, so long as subalterns continue to believe in the possibility of force. Threats of force can be combined with the occasional use of actual force to reinforce their credibility. Punishment, suppression, torture, and other forms of force, then, can be employed as a last resort, exercised mainly when the threat of force is challenged (Wrong 1979: 41; Wartenberg 1990: 96). The need for the occasional use of force shows that a structure of power based on threats alone cannot be fully effective. Subalterns must believe in the willingness and ability of a principal to use the threatened force, and a coercive structure of leadership cannot be sustained unless a principal does occasionally exercise some actual force.

The actual capacity to exercise force may not, of course, match the threats that are made – a principal may lack the necessary physical resources or be unwilling to use them to the full. This points to the fact that coercion, which rests on a pattern of threat and credibility, may become very unstable in the face of a direct and concerted challenge. Continued obedience by subalterns depends not so much on the per-ceived severity of the force, as on a belief in the certainty that it will be used. If subalterns believe that force will not be used, or will not be used on the scale that is threatened, then they will be more likely to mount a challenge to the principal's power (Wrong 1979: 43–4). Conversely, threats may be very effective if subalterns have an exaggerated impression of the principal's ability to act. Subalterns may, for example, overestimate the physical resources that are available or the willingness of their principals to use them (Wartenberg 1990: 101).

While force is predominantly negative, coercion can be positive as well as negative. Through coercion it is possible to get a subaltern to do something as well as to prevent them from doing it. This is because 'the logic of a threat is precisely its positing action that an agent is able to forestall by acting in an appropriate manner' (Wartenberg 1990:101; see also Tilly 1990: 19). Coercion shares with force, however, the likelihood that it will be experienced in alienating ways, and so it is especially likely to engender resistance. Thus, Etzioni (1961) holds that coercive structures of power are especially likely to be associated with an 'alienative involvement' on the part of subalterns, and he cites the examples of economic exploitation, slavery, and prison regimes.

Leadership through inducement involves the manipulation of agents through the offering of rewards for conformity. People are offered varying incentives to act in one way or another, leaving subalterns with a deliberately constrained choice of action alternatives. Inducement was seen by Machiavelli and Pareto as characteristic of the 'foxes' of political life, those who rely on cunning and intrigue to sustain their power. Where coercion rests on threats and may have a limited degree of stability, even without the occasional use of force, a reliance on the promise of rewards can be effective only for so long as there are, in fact, regular pay-outs of these rewards. Unless the promised rewards are forthcoming, obedience will not continue. For this reason, a stable structure of inducement requires the constant replenishment of the resources that make the rewards possible or, more unusually, a complete monopoly of a virtually inexhaustible resource. Etzioni (1961) sees such 'remunerative' power as generating a 'calculative involvement' on the part of subalterns: involvement in the maintenance of the power relationship is intrinsically neither negative nor positive, but depends upon a recurrent calculation of the advantages and disadvantages that it offers. Arendt (1970) saw coercion and inducement as forms of the negative, destructive type of power that she called 'violence', using the word in a broader sense than is usual.

The non-delivery of any promised rewards is likely to be experienced by subalterns as a deprivation of what they have come to regard as an entitlement, and a relation of inducement may all too easily switch over into one of perceived coercion. In this respect, coercion and inducement can be seen as complementary aspects of a strategic, instrumental usage of resources. They operate, respectively, through the punishments and the rewards that can be attached to alternative courses of action, and they depend on the willingness of actors to calculate the profits and losses that are associated with these alternatives.

Domination through command rests on the idea of the *right* to give orders and a corresponding *obligation* to obey. There is willing compliance on the part of a subaltern because of a commitment to the legitimacy of the source of the command, not because of an independent and autonomous evaluation of its content. While coercion and inducement are characteristic of those whom Pareto describes, using the language of fables and fairy tales, as the lions and the foxes, command might be said to be characteristic of the domineering but benign 'bears'. Power is legitimate because it is accepted as being right, correct, justified, or valid in some way (Held 1989: 102; Beetham 1991: 10–12). This legitimacy flows from the internalisation of significant cultural meanings and an identification with those who are seen as their guardians or guarantors because of the positions that they occupy through election, appointment, or some other accepted procedure. The values to which principals and subalterns orient themselves underpin the norms that define the various institutionalised social positions to which rights and obligations are attached. What is usually called 'authority' exists 'whenever one, several, or many people explicitly or tacitly permit someone else to make decisions for them for some category of acts' (Lindblom 1977: 17–18).

Some analysts have seen command as requiring that there be a value consensus between principals and subalterns (Lipset 1959; Almond and Verba 1963). Where there is such a shared moral commitment to the substantive values that lie behind particular commands, rather than simply to the formal procedural principles through which the commands are issued, a structure of authority is, of course, likely to be particularly strong. This is, however, at the margins of command, which can exist with much lower levels of consensus.

Although command rests on the willing compliance of the subalterns, they do not accord or deny legitimacy to particular commands at will. The normative framework is – from the standpoint of any individual subaltern – both mandatory and compulsory. It is, in Durkheim's (1895) sense, a social fact. Individual agents may, therefore, act altruistically in the interests of others, and contrary to their own interests, despite the fact that they disapprove of the contents of the particular commands that they have been given. This relative detachment from the consequences or outcomes of acts of legitimate domination is the principal reason why coercion or inducement will normally underpin the patterns of command that are found in particular societies.

The relationship between command and corrective influence has been highlighted by James Scott (1990) in his elaboration of Mosca's idea of the political formula. He argues that relations of domination can secure a legitimacy through the particular 'public transcripts' that both justify and mask the realities of coercion and inducement that underpin political leadership. A public transcript is a narrative or account constructed in accordance with a 'script' that is provided by the particular form of discourse that underpins a power relationship. Domination is strengthened to the extent that subalterns accept this narrative as a rationalisation of their reasons for acting:

> The theatrical imperatives that normally prevail in situations of domination produce a public transcript in close conformity with how the dominant group would wish to have things appear. The dominant never control the stage absolutely, but their wishes normally prevail. In the short run, it is in the interests of the subordinate to produce a more or less credible performance, speaking

the lines and making the gestures he [*sic*] knows are
expected of him. (James Scott 1990: 4; see also Newby
1975)

In a situation of command, then, the public transcript is
systematically skewed towards the interests of the principal,
reflecting the incorporation of the subaltern into the dominant discourse. The coexistence of command with coercion
and inducement is apparent in the existence of what Scott
calls the 'hidden transcripts' through which subalterns, in
private, contradict or inflect what appears in the public
transcript. Such hidden transcripts are produced by subalterns for an audience of friends and intimates who they
regard as equals, or who are not directly involved in the
power relationship.

Positions of command require explicit, overt, and sustained action on the part of the principal, as the dominant
agent must, at the very least, make the order known to those
who are expected to obey. What I shall call constraint,
however, brings together inducement and anticipated coercion, and it may occur without any explicit intervention by
a principal. A constraining actor has superior resources and
is able to restrict the autonomy of others by limiting the
range of options that can be considered as feasible courses of
action. This restriction may occur without the constraining
actor showing any direct intent to influence the others. A
monopoly supplier of credit, for example, can limit the power
and autonomy of those who seek to borrow, simply because
they have few alternative sources of capital open to them. The
interests of the participants converge around a structure of
power in which a constraining principal faces a tightly constrained subaltern. There is, of course, a fuzzy boundary
between constraint and command, especially where actors
obey through an anticipatory reaction. In such a situation,
those in command may not have explicitly voiced an order,
but their subordinates obey their anticipated wishes
nevertheless.

The final form of domination to be considered is what I
have called expertise. This occurs when cognitive symbols are
structured into organised bodies of knowledge in terms of
which some people are regarded as experts and others defer

to their superior knowledge and skills. This type of power is based on trust in a principal's specialised knowledge or skill rather than the specific social position that they hold in a structure of command. Employing the language of fable and fairy tale once more, expertise might be said to be characteristic of the wise 'owls'. It is a form of domination that rests upon specific knowledge or wisdom accepted on trust by a subaltern. The authority of a doctor over a patient, for example, is, ideal typically, based on their possession of a specialised technical competence in medical matters to which the patient defers.[10] Rational deliberation, free from power, occurs when a person's acceptance of an order is based on an independent, knowledgeable, and reasoned assessment of its content. Expertise, however, is a form of persuasive influence and rests on a substantive *trust* in the competence of the person issuing an order (Wartenberg 1990: 54) and a corresponding acceptance of one's own lack of competence. Patients, for example, typically have no significant technical knowledge about their medical conditions and so cannot be persuaded of the truth of what a doctor says simply through rational dialogue and debate. This is why they are 'patients', passive agents. They must have faith in the competence of the expert, because they have not personally evaluated the particular grounds for the advice they are given. The expert, for his or her part, may try to ensure that their technical knowledge remains an esoteric monopoly, seeking to avoid the possibility that subalterns may challenge them. This may involve combining expertise with manipulation.

Structures of command and expertise involve a degree of 'moral involvement' by subalterns in their own subordination. Subaltern involvement, Etzioni (1961) argued, is both intense and positive, and this relationship is epitomised by the devoted party member or the loyal follower. This moral involvement contrasts with the alienative involvement that typically occurs in structures of coercion and inducement.

Coercion, inducement, command, and expertise rarely appear in their pure forms, they are ideal typical forms of domination. The power relations of any actual society are organised through its institutional structures into a variety of concrete combinations of power that combine these types in complex ways. States, business enterprises, universities, churches, families, and gangs, for example, combine the different forms of power to form the concrete patterns of power that give them their specific characteristics.

Empirical studies of power have commonly distinguished between economic, political, and ideological domination as the most distinctive combinations of these forms of power (Mann 1986b: 22–3; Gellner 1988; Runciman 1989: 12). Political domination has its particular focus in state institutions, its core elements being the processes of authoritative domination that give rise to structures of command. As a sovereign organisation of command within a particular territory, a state is organised around the specialised structure of coercive agencies and mechanisms that Althusser (1971) called 'repressive apparatuses', but it is also closely associated with what he called 'ideological apparatuses'. It is through these ideological apparatuses that state legitimation occurs. Mann has separated the coercive aspects of state institutions from their command aspects in his distinction between 'military power' and the narrower civil form of political power. It is principally in the modern societies of the West that this structural separation of the military and the civil aspects of political domination has been developed to any extent (see also Giddens 1985: 288).

Command relations themselves, however, are not confined to states and their political institutions. Business enterprises, churches, schools, and other associations of modern societies are all organised around the exercise of command. Managerial hierarchies of command are the means through which these organisations control their members and relate to other organisations through inter-organisational coalitions and alliances. Inter-enterprise relations in business, however, may also be organised as 'economic' relations of inducement. The offering or withholding of credit, for example, is a means through which one enterprise can influence the options that are open to another. The activities of business enterprises are the basis of the economic relations through which economic domination is produced. This economic domination is rooted most directly in processes of allocative domination in so far as it involves the calculative use of material resources, generally in the form of the 'wealth' possessed by economic agents, in exchange and market relations. While economic domination, operating through relations of inducement, rests on what Weber called 'domination by virtue of a constellation of interests', the latter is not exclusively economic in character and I will show that it is important to recognise a number of forms of such constraint.[11]

What is often called 'ideological domination', finally, involves the symbolic resources that enter into signification and legitimation, and that are the bases of conceptions of social status. Some have described this as 'symbolic power' (Thompson 1995: 16–17), 'cultural and social power' (Jessop 1972: 58), or 'normative power' (Etzioni 1961: 11). This form of domination is rooted in those ideological apparatuses that Althusser saw as central to the generation of legitimacy.

This distinction between economic, political, and ideological domination, then, is a useful basis for empirical investigations of concrete configurations of power, and I shall make many references to economic and political domination, in particular, in the course of this book. In developing my argument I will emphasise the interdependence and combination of forms of power in specific acts of power. Although they can, for analytical purposes, be discussed in isolation from each other, they generally occur in specific, concrete combinations. As the argument of the book develops, therefore, the later chapters explore common patterns of articulation while focusing on particular forms of power. I do not discuss each aspect of power as a separate analytical dimension, but in relation to the concrete structures of power in which it occurs. Command cannot be considered in isolation from coercion, and constraint can only be understood if seen in relation to legitimation and consent.

Counteraction

I have argued that power always involves resistance, and particularly important forms of resistance arise in and around structures of domination. Elementary forms of counteraction may be purely individual responses to domination, as occurs with inchoate resentment, hostility, or withdrawal, or in isolated acts of disruption or sabotage. Fully developed counteraction, however, is co-ordinated or collective action against the leadership. It occurs where resources and commitments are mobilised for the pursuit of shared goals and interests and put to use in struggles against the established leadership (Tilly 1978: 7). Such counteracting power derives its strength from the number of subalterns that it involves and the solidarity that they are able to achieve in mobilising their resources. It results from a shared sense of opposition or contention and is a collective attempt to influence the holding and exercising of sovereign power. It is, in one sense, power from below rather than power from above.

Counteraction takes two principal forms. When oppositional action is institutionalised and counteracting groups are recognised by the established leadership, they are seen as legitimate 'members' of a larger system of action around the structure of domination. Charles Tilly holds that, in the case of state power, 'At any point in time, some (and only some) of the contenders have achieved recognition of their collective rights to wield power over the government, and have developed routine ways of exercising those rights. They are *members of the polity*' (Tilly 1978: 125). That is, they are members of the political system, but not of the state itself. They are a part of the recognised and legitimate political process, but they are not an integral part of the state. They do, nevertheless, have a routine and institutionalised place in the making of decisions, competing with other such groups for influence in relation to state policies. This form of counteraction can best be described as 'pressure'. Modern states have increasingly come to be surrounded by structures of pressure that mediate between them and their citizens and that constitute the complex polities or political systems within which authority is exercised.

Those counteracting groups that do not become a part of the institutional structure of established power, on the other hand, are not 'members' of it. They 'contend without routine or recognition' (Tilly 1978: 125). These are the 'challengers' that seek to restructure a pattern of domination and to enhance their own power position, either through a claim to recognition for themselves, or through more radical reorganisations of power. Challengers may oppose the existing members of the established power structure, or they may work with some of them to secure their own larger goals. They exercise protest rather than pressure, relying on coercion and inducement to make their views felt.

What have been called social movements are complex alliances of member and challenger groups that are organised for counteraction. While many social movements do embrace both member and challenger groups, others are movements of protest that rely almost exclusively on challenger groups rather than those that seek to operate through conventional pressure politics.

Pressure and protest, then, are the two principal forms of counteraction. Counteraction, like domination, is at its most effective when it draws on and makes explicit the hidden transcripts employed by subalterns. Protest, for example, is organised as effective collective action through the construction of autonomous identities and forms of consciousness that overtly challenge the public transcripts of the principals. These public transcripts may define protesters in derogatory terms as, for example, a 'mob' or a 'rabble'. At its strongest, protest must involve the construction of what Gramsci (1926–37) called a 'counter hegemony' to the dominant discourses and their transcripts.

Pressure, understood as an assertion of the wish or demand to be heard by those who dominate, is to be seen as a recognised or institutionalised form of counteraction against those with the power of command. Those who attempt to exercise pressure have no right to command others to take their views into account or to have their preferences translated directly into action. Nevertheless, they use persuasive influence and forms of inducement in order to push for their views to be taken into account by those who do have the power of command, and they have resources to make this pressure more or less effective. Command and pressure may, of course, shade over into one another. Corporatist practices on the part of a government, for example, may involve the delegation of certain powers of command to pressure groups, so incorporating them into a formal structure of authority. This was, for example, a key feature of the fascist regimes of Europe in the 1930s.

Protest is subaltern resistance that is exercised as a counter-mobilisation to the existing structure of domination. Where pressure on state power involves the attempt to influence and lobby for a particular outcome from within a political system, protest involves entering into a contest or trial of strength that challenges an existing structure of domination and attempts to restructure it in some way. This protest is expressed most effectively as the collective action of organisations and social movements.

Interpersonal Power

I have, so far, concentrated on large-scale structures of power and resistance, of domination and counteraction. Power also exists, however, in a whole range of interpersonal situations where individuals significantly influence each other. This is the form of power that Weber recognised as occurring throughout society 'in the drawing room as well as in a market, from the rostrum of a lecture-hall as well as from the command post of a regiment, from an erotic or charitable relationship as well as from scholarly discussion or athletics'. It is the power inherent in the relations of parents to children, the relations of playmates, lovers, friends, and acquaintances (Weber 1914: 943; see also Mannheim 1947: 49–51).

Interpersonal power is rooted in face-to-face contexts of interaction. It is based not on the content or source of an order, but on the personal attributes of the individual making it as these are perceived by individuals who have a direct knowledge of one another. People are able to relate to each other as individual selves, and not simply as the occupants of social positions with authorised or delegated powers. Interpersonal power operates through the personal resources of physique and personality that individuals bring to their encounters and through the various resources on which some depend and to which others can give access. It is in this way that one person can make another bend to her or his will and so become a principal in an interpersonal power relationship.

Self and identity are *embodied* phenomena, and it is their bodily characteristics that allow individuals to enter into social relations or that lead to their social exclusion. At the same time, however, individuals are able to monitor and, therefore, to control, their bodily actions: they are able, within limits, to choose the ways in which they present their body – and, therefore, their self – in everyday encounters. Self-presentations are constructed through the shared cultural meanings available to people and so tend to be more or less conventionalised within a society (Goffman 1959). What is commonly called 'body language' is but a partial recognition of this wider process of self-presentation.

What Goffman called the 'interaction order' arises from the mutual self-presentations of embodied individuals as they construct and reconstruct their identities and life plans in response to each other. It consists of a complex of everyday encounters that may become more or less routinised. Once negotiated, individual encounters do not usually need to be renegotiated. They are, rather, subject to constant marginal transformations of reciprocal expectations that are largely taken for granted by the participants. One part of the expectations that people share may be the institutionalised roles that they occupy and the authority that this gives them, but Goffman's point is that all such role relationships involve the proximal dynamics of self-presentations from which they can, for analytical purposes, be distinguished.

Virtually all social relations are manifested through the face-to-face relations of particular individuals, and it is here that the myriad and diffuse power relations that Weber identified have their effect. Weber did not, however, provide a systematic or even useful account of interpersonal power, and the work of Foucault has been particularly influential in providing a basis for this. In his concern for the body and subjectivity as the objects of power relations, Foucault has complemented the work of Goffman and provided the basis for a sophisticated reformulation of a long-standing line of research on micropower.

Interpersonal power is at its strongest in the proximal contexts of face-to-face encounters, but it is not limited to these. More important than physical presence is the temporal and spatial availability of others in a locale, even though they may not currently be physically present (Giddens 1979: 207). Interpersonal power does, nevertheless, become more attenuated as time–space distanciation alters. The introduction of writing and of the means of distributing it physically and electronically increases the scope of interpersonal power. Electronic media of communication make it possible to sustain some forms of interpersonal power over greater distances, while reducing the time that this takes to the virtually instantaneous scale of face-to-face encounters. At the same time, interpersonal power is assimilated ever more into structures of domination: individuals encounter one another more as the 'disembodied' occupants of social positions than as concrete and particular individuals. What Weber called 'charismatic power', for example, is rooted in the strength of individual personality and is more difficult to sustain as the size of a group increases and the opportunities for direct face-to-face encounters diminish. Charisma loses many of its distinctive characteristics and is embedded in more routine structures of power.

Personal traits and capacities, and the subjective assessments that are made of them, cannot be separated from the forms of domination and counteraction that I have discussed. A parent exercises interpersonal power over a child, but also has certain legal rights that the child may grow up to accept and that will be recognised by others. Equally, the interpersonal power relations between a husband and a wife are affected by the legal rights and responsibilities of each of them in the wider political and economic structures in which they are involved. Similarly, it is important to recognise that the relations between nation states or large business enterprises are manifested in and through the interpersonal encounters of their presidents, chief executives, and other holders of authority. This interpersonal power has to be seen in relation to the production and reproduction of structures of domination. As Foucault recognised: 'If we speak of structures or mechanisms of power, it is only insofar as we suppose that certain persons exercise power over others' (Foucault 1982: 225).

2
Command and Sovereign Power

The aspect of domination that I have called 'command' is concerned with formal structures of authority that are organised through structures of legitimacy and the value commitments that underpin them. Particular individuals are 'authorised' to issue orders and decisions, and they expect compliance or obedience from others: the principals have the right to direct the actions of subaltern others (Weber 1914: 943). The powers of command are the formal powers of decision-making that are attached to particular social positions. States are and have been among the most important of these authoritarian organisations, but positions of command can exist in any sovereign, hierarchical organisation: in business enterprises, churches, universities, and many other formal associations. In each case, however, characteristic legal forms are involved in constituting positions of authority.

Positions of command are the bases for the formation of elites. The word 'elite' has been used very loosely to refer to superior social groups of many different kinds: upper classes, status groups, the wealthy, the intelligent, or merely the prominent. Within a broad tradition of elite theory in social science, however, the term has most commonly and usefully been employed to refer to positions of command in organisations and those who occupy them. There can, then, be as many kinds of elite as there are authoritarian organisations: state elites, business elites, church elites, university elites, and so on. In addition to the study of these separate elites, there has been much research on the extent to which those who head the various hierarchies of authority in a society are connected into larger social elites. For example, the top positions within particular business enterprises (their directors and top executives) may be linked into larger business or corporate elites that exercise powers of command across broad sectors of an economy. Similarly, those who occupy positions at the top of the separate institutional hierarchies within a state (the government, senior civil servants, top military officers, etc.) may be connected into an overarching state elite. Where such corporate and state elites are formed, it is also possible to see whether they are connected into a single, all-embracing 'power elite' that exercises its powers of command across the whole society.

It has sometimes been said that finding an overall elite in a complex, hierarchical society is hardly surprising: wherever hierarchies exist, it is possible to identify their top positions, and to call the set of all top positions an 'elite' is to overstate the case. However, a purely abstract elite is simply the starting point for elite analysis proper. True elites have more than a merely formal or nominal existence, and they may show the kind of solidarity and consciousness that makes them real social groups capable of acting in common. Empirical research on elites has explored the extent to which hierarchies of authority are, in fact, connected into overlapping structures through cohesive bonds of social solidarity. This involves investigating patterns of recruitment into positions of command and the mechanisms of integration that link their occupants.

This chapter begins with a discussion of command and elites within modern states, and it goes on to explore the formation of economic elites. In each case, I will look at the ways in which researchers have tried to highlight the roles played by state and corporate elites in modern societies and whether these are, indeed, forged together into a single power elite.

States and State Elites

States are organised around the holding and exercise of legitimate authority. They are collective entities whose rule over particular territories is maintained by their leaders, or 'masters', and their administrative servants (Weber 1914: 952). A state is, in the words of Held (1989: 11), 'a legally circumscribed structure of power with supreme jurisdiction over a territory'. This legitimate authority rests on physical force and the threat of its use in support of authoritative commands. It is for this reason that Tilly has argued that a state must be seen as the paramount 'coercion-wielding organisation' within a specific territory (Tilly 1990: 1; see also de Jouvenel 1945). States govern their territories through more or less coherent sets of administrative organs that can be described as their 'state apparatuses'. These involve the executive, legislative, administrative, judicial, and repressive organs through which the surveillance and control of those who live within the state's jurisdiction are ensured. The sphere of the state may also include other dependent but constitutionally separate agencies concerned with education, health, welfare, transport, finance, and other services and activities. While some of these have been seen as forming specifically 'ideological' state apparatuses (Althusser 1971), they do not form a structural part of a state unless they are constitutionally recognised as such.

Modern states can be seen in terms of six defining characteristics:

- Territorial sovereignty
- Organised violence
- Constitutional legality
- Citizenship rights
- Fiscal management
- Rational bureaucracy[1]

When states occupy clearly defined physical spaces and claim full authority in relation to the other states with which they coexist, they have territorial sovereignty. They have frontiers or borders across which the movement or migration of peoples is regulated, and they claim sovereign jurisdiction over those who live within these borders. They assert their right to close their own borders and to enforce entry or exit through the use of passports, visas, and physical controls.

Organised violence is the basis of the force that is organised into standing armies and police forces and that enables modern states to make their commands effective in the face of deviance and disobedience. Force is neither the normal nor the only means of state power, but it is the *specific* means through which, as a last resort, a state can enforce its sovereignty (Weber 1914). Although some have seen a state solely as an instrument of force and coercion, no state can operate through force alone. At the very least, members of a state apparatus must themselves be committed to the system, and even Mosca recognised that legitimacy (advanced through a 'political formula') is not a mere mask for coercion but reflects the genuine introduction of moral principles into the question of state power (Mosca 1896: 71; Wrong 1979: 104).

It is constitutional legality that provides a structure of legitimacy for state coercion and for its other political and administrative procedures.[2] This is the 'rule of law', the impersonal and formally impartial legal procedures that can be changed only by legislation and through which modern states operate.

Citizenship rights, and the corresponding obligations, define the participation of a society's members in its political and legal systems, economic organisations, and systems of welfare provision. In many, though not all, cases citizenship is tied to the idea of nationality, through which ethnic, religious, or cultural identity is defined. Even where no strong idea of nationhood exists, the language of 'nation' and 'national' is almost invariably tied to the idea of the territorial state, and modern states regard themselves as nation states. Such states operate in relation to national economies and societies, whose members are, nevertheless, increasingly involved in international and transnational structures and processes. Rights have increasingly been cast as 'human rights' that transcend nation-state boundaries and have a universal significance that must be defended through non-national agencies (Soysal 1994).

Fiscal management is the means through which a large state can finance its apparatuses and can promote the various interests and demands of its citizens. It must secure the necessary resources through taxation and borrowing, and while the need to secure a tax revenue is a feature of all states, the scale of social expenditure in modern states makes effective fiscal management critical for them. This has centred around the level of the 'tax burden' that can legitimately be imposed on members to meet the various spending demands. The modern state is what Schumpeter (1954) called a 'tax state'.

Rational bureaucracy is the counterpart to constitutional legality. At its most general, a bureaucracy is simply administration by officials who occupy positions of command because they have been appointed rather than elected. The exercise of command in a modern state depends on structures of impersonal, rationally regulated, bureaucratic administration.

Weber contrasted this rational form of administration with the 'traditional' forms characteristic of pre-modern states, which he saw as having their institutional bases in long-standing custom and practice. A modern bureaucracy is a technical, formally rational system of administration based on the employment of full-time officials who do not own the means of administration and cannot appropriate their powers of command. Bureaucrats are salaried officials, not personal retainers, and they work full-time in a vocation with tenure for life. The work of officials is formed into a hierarchy of clearly defined responsibilities, and their giving of orders is limited to their particular areas of jurisdiction. Officials depend on written documents and a subordinate staff of clerks to maintain them (Weber 1914: 956–63). Higher officials supervise lower ones, and all are selected and promoted on the basis of their specialist training and competence. The decisive reason for the growth of bureaucracy, held Weber, is its technical superiority over other forms of administration (Weber 1914: 973). It is a structure of command that makes possible a systematic and rational process of administration.

Weber saw states as organised around an institutionalised division between the 'rulers' and the 'ruled'. The rulers are those who have the right to demand particular forms of behaviour from others. Their orders are taken into account in some way by the ruled and become an important factor in their choice of how to act. In the strongest case, this will involve complete conformity with the commands of the rulers. In weaker cases, the ruled may simply treat the commands of the rulers as necessary variables in their calculus of action. This division between rulers and ruled is the basis of the various elite theories, the earliest attempts to link the formation of ruling minorities directly to institutionalised positions of command being Weber's account of bureaucracy and Michel's work on organisational oligarchy (see Burnham 1943). It was, however, Mills (1956) who did the most to popularise the concept of an elite as the holders of top positions of command. Putnam (1976: 11–12) has usefully distinguished the state elite of 'proximate decision-makers' from the 'intermediate' levels of command (Giddens 1973) that lie between it and the lower levels of power.

As I have already noted, it is important to look empirically at the extent to which the elites at the heads of the hierarchies that make up a modern state do, in fact, overlap to form a single state elite that can act as a single, unified agency with a coherent policy or programme. Among the most important of these specialised elites within a modern state are:

- *Legislative elites.* These are based in an assembly or assemblies that have the constitutional authority to enact laws. They include such groups as Members of Parliament (MPs) and Members of the House of Lords in Britain, Senators and Congressional Members in the United States, and members of other, similar national legislatures.
- *Government or executive elites.* These are the cabinet and ministerial teams that are put together by monarchs, presidents, or prime ministers. In systems such as Britain, the Government is drawn almost exclusively from the legislative elite, while in some presidential systems, such

as the United States, there is an almost complete formal separation of the executive from the legislature.

- *Administrative elites.* These are the top civil servants and other bureaucrats who administer and monitor the implementation of laws and government decisions. A civil service tends to be organised into a number of separate branches, some of which may be organised as semi-private agencies that work for the state under contract (for example, the Office of the Rail Regulator in Britain).

- *Judicial elites.* These hold power in senior courts of law that decide the interpretation and application of laws and that are involved in appeals against the decisions of lower courts and in the making of constitutional adjudications.

- *Local state elites.* These elites are based in the legislative and administrative structures of the local or regional branches of a state. This includes devolved and regional assemblies, constituent assemblies in federal states, and some more localised structures of authority. These are by far the most diverse and fragmented of all elites because of their geographical basis.

- *Military elites.* While the executive, legislative, and judicial hierarchies are central to the authoritarian aspects of states, the military and police hierarchies are central to their coercive apparatuses. Military elites are officers of the rank of general and above who hold the leading positions in regiments and operational forces, and who are involved in the planning and execution of military actions in central military agencies such as those centred on the Pentagon in the United States and the Ministry of Defence in Britain.

- *Police and para-police elites.* These include the senior levels of the police forces and security services that make the major strategic decisions about crime and espionage control operations and whose occupants are involved in the formulation of national policing, prison, and security policies. This includes national and federal bodies such as the CIA and FBI in the United States, MI5 and MI6 in Britain, national police forces, and topmost levels in the prison and sub-national police services.[3]

Integration and Recruitment

Mills' classic study (1956) of the power elite in the United States set the scene for all later research into the formation of elites. He sought to show that the state elite was part of a larger 'power elite' that embraced all the strategic hierarchies of contemporary American society, inside and outside the state, and that these hierarchies formed a centralised structure of power through the overlapping and interlocking of positions among them.

Mills recognised that not all branches of the US state carried equal weight in the distribution of power, and he gave particular attention to its military arm – the 'warlords' – and what he called the 'political directorate'. This latter category included the executive elite and many of those in the legislative, judicial, and administrative elites, but it did not include ordinary members of Congress or the local state elites. The question of how broadly to delimit a particular elite for study has been a matter of hot debate, and there is no general solution to the question. The drawing of boundaries is always a matter for judgement on the part of the researcher as to what makes sense in the particular situation being studied.

Mills saw the structure of command within US society as a whole as defined by a triangle of power that connected the political directorate, the warlords, and those he called the 'corporate rich'.[4] A single and cohesive power elite exists, he held, where the various elites do not form discrete clusters located in their separate hierarchies of command but are fused together through tight patterns of circulation and association. Mills explored this through measures of social background and by directly investigating the overlapping and interlocking of top positions. Using some basic techniques of social network analysis (Scott 2000b), Mills showed that there was, indeed, an interlocking of positions into a single 'directorate' of power. This power elite, he argued, had the potential to decide all strategic matters of state policy, even if its members did not actually and routinely exercise these powers on a day-to-day basis.

Mills probably overstated the implications of his findings. While he had shown that those in positions of command had the *potential* to act in a unified and co-ordinated way to secure their own advantages, he did not demonstrate that there were no obstacles to the exercise of this potential. In practice, members of a state elite respond to pressure and protest or may simply allow events to develop without intervening. Elitist studies simply show the ways in which the capacity for command is organised, and they suggest that whenever this capacity is exercised it can, if necessary, be enforced through the legitimate use of the coercive apparatuses of the state. Mills' frequently challenged gloss on this was that the members of the US power elite did actually exercise their capacity to secure their own interests.

This style of elite research – often called power structure research (Domhoff 1980) – rests on the methodology of positional analysis. In such research, the top positions in the most salient agencies of a state are identified and the interconnections among them are mapped in terms of their *integration* and their *recruitment*. Elite integration is measured by the extent of any interlocking and interchanging of persons among elite positions. 'Interlocking' refers to interconnections that result when elite members hold multiple positions within the elite; 'interchange' refers to interconnections that result from career mobility and movement among elite positions. 'Recruitment' differences are apparent in the social background of elite members, and this is generally measured by their homogeneity in terms of class, gender, ethnicity, age, education, and other demographic variables. Recruitment studies show the 'regimes of recruitment' that operate in a society.[5]

Regimes of recruitment vary in their openness and in the degree of structural segregation that exists among the top positions. An elite is open when it is relatively easy for those from outside a dominant social category to enter top positions of command. These positions are marked by segregation when entry into certain areas of command is limited to those from particular social backgrounds. Recruitment to elite positions may, for example, be overwhelmingly monopolised by men, though women may be able to enter – and perhaps be disproportionately represented in – certain sections.

Regimes of recruitment are shaped by both 'supply' and 'demand' factors. The supply of potential recruits from particular social backgrounds may be limited by the material advantages and disadvantages that they experience, and by the other relational constraints under which they live. This would involve a 'structural selection' of possible entrants on the basis of their economic and social capital. The demand for those of a particular type, on the other hand, reflects the judgements made by those who do the recruiting. The gatekeepers who regulate the pathways of entry to elite positions are the electors and selectors who choose recruits at various stages of entry, and they may show a bias in the qualifications that they look for. As Putnam has argued: 'The pathway into the political elite is blocked by a series of gates, and the gatekeepers may consider candidates' social backgrounds' (Putnam 1976: 39; see also Norris and Lovenduski 1995: 106ff).

Connell (1987: 151–5; see also Holloway 1994) has highlighted the particular importance of gendered regimes of recruitment in modern states. These are, he argues, typically organised around both a gendered division of labour that also involves a gendered hierarchy of authority. Recruitment to state elites is disproportionately male, with men predominating, in particular, in the legislative, executive, and repressive arms. The proportion of women elected as MPs in Britain never rose above 5 per cent over the whole period between 1918 (when women were first given the right to vote) and 1983. The figure rose slowly to 9.2 per cent by 1992 and peaked at 18.4 per cent in 1997 (Norris and Lovenduski 1995). The high level of exclusion of women from elite positions, Connell suggests, may be associated with a segregation by gender at the intermediate levels of command. While men continue to be strongly represented in most elite and intermediate positions, women can achieve relatively high levels of representation at the intermediate levels of state apparatuses concerned with health, education, and welfare. Even in these areas, however, male dominance increases with each step in the hierarchy. In the British state elite at the end of the twentieth century, for example, women made up fewer than 10 per cent of top civil servants, and fewer than 5 per cent of the very top grades. The percentage of women varied from none at all in the Inland Revenue, the Northern Ireland Office, and Government Communications Headquarters

(GCHQ), through less than 10 per cent in the Cabinet Office, the Department of Trade, and the Department for Education, to almost one-third in the Department of Social Security and the Office of Population Censuses and Surveys (Puwar 2000: 134–5).[6]

A gendered regime of recruitment, Connell argues, is often associated with a 'gendered structure of cathexis'. In such a structure, the subordinate emotional labour (Hochschild 1983) of women in intermediate and less salient positions becomes an important support for male power in those areas, while the top positions themselves are organised around strongly masculine norms of sociability.[7] – In the British legislative elite the dominance of men, the organisation of parliamentary activities in relation to male careers outside Parliament, and the ways in which social life in Parliament is organised around the bars all reinforce a masculine world view (Puwar 2000). Women are regarded by the men – and many women take this same view of themselves – as 'space invaders'. They are, literally, out of place in the elite social space that is run by and for men.

Ethnic regimes of recruitment in contemporary states also show a great disproportionality between the various ethnic groups. There had been only three non-white MPs in Britain prior to 1987, though there had been a significant number of Jewish MPs since the late nineteenth century. The number of black and Asian parliamentary candidates increased in 1979, and the number of non-white MPs rose to nine in 1997. In the Civil Service, the number of black and Asian recruits amounted to just 2.4 per cent of all Civil Servants at Grade Seven or above: there was only one above Grade Four (Norris and Lovenduski 1995: 103–4; Puwar 2000: 214). At this time, these groups accounted for about 5 per cent of the total population.

Zweigenhaft and Domhoff (1982, 1991) looked at Jews and African Americans, finding that, despite programmes of positive action, the US state elite was characterised by the institutional racism diagnosed by Stokely Carmichael (Carmichael and Hamilton 1967). African Americans, in particular, experienced their life as space invaders in white institutions if they managed to enter elite positions, and they never rose to the very highest levels (Landry 1987).

Perhaps the greatest amount of research effort has been devoted to the investigation of class regimes of recruitment, following the lead of Mills himself. The vast majority of members of the legislature in the United States, Britain, Italy, and West Germany came from the higher managerial and professional occupations of Goldthorpe's (1980) Class I. Typically, around 5 per cent of the population are members of this class, but their representation within the state elites varied from five to eleven times this figure (Putnam 1976: 22–7).

For those from manual and lower white-collar backgrounds, it was almost impossible to enter top positions of command unless they had a higher education. In Italy and Germany, those with degrees are over-represented among top civil servants by a factor of thirty. Oxford and Cambridge graduates in Britain in the 1970s accounted for one-third of MPs, two-thirds of non-Cabinet ministers, and three-quarters of Cabinet Ministers: less than one per cent of the total population were Oxford or Cambridge graduates. This pattern is typical for class regimes of recruitment (see, for example, Guttsman 1963; Domhoff 1971; Boyd 1973; Whitley et al. 1981; Bottomore and Brym 1989; Scott 1991b).

This research has been used to suggest that class regimes of recruitment offer prima-facie evidence for the existence of a ruling class. Domhoff (1967, 1979, 1998) in the United States and Scott (1991b) and Miliband (1969) in Britain, for example, have argued that the evidence shows that capitalist classes are disproportionately represented in state elites and, as Mills showed, that they have the capacity for unified command.

It is through investigations into elite integration and recruitment that the structure of cohesion or solidarity among those in positions of command can be shown and related to the larger structures within which the formal positions are embedded. This research suggests how likely it is that there will be any common outlook among those in elite positions and so suggests the direction of any bias that might be expected in their policy deliberations and decisions. Meisel (1958) has suggested that an account of elite integration and recruitment must also be concerned with the extent to which what he calls the 'three Cs' – cohesion, consciousness, and conspiracy – have been developed. A strong elite is cohesively integrated, has a shared consciousness or outlook on the world, and is involved in co-operative and collusive actions that carry forward this consciousness. Meisel holds that these are always empirical matters and cannot simply be read off from measures of integration and recruitment alone. Studies of the state elite in the United States, for example, have shown that patterns of interaction and informal association are shaped by the overlapping and interlocking of personnel in elite positions and so establish the basis for shared values and outlook. Its members socialise regularly at Georgetown cocktail parties, at social clubs and retreats, and at numerous other places where they can discuss common concerns and forge their preferred policies (Domhoff 1974).

Economic Governance

Economic command within a capitalist society depends on legally constituted powers of authority structured through relations of property ownership. Company law, the law of property, and the law of contract are the principal legal institutions that define the corporate forms taken by capitalist enterprise, and the similar legal frameworks of business that are found in the leading capitalist economies give a degree of similarity to their structures of command. Patterns of property ownership have changed, however, and the debate over corporate governance has focused on the implications of this for the structure of command.

Modern corporate organisation involves the formation of undertakings into legal entities called companies or corporations.[8] – A company is the legal owner of business assets and is the employer of those who work on them. Decisions about the use of the assets and employees, however, are taken by its directors and their appointed managers, whose legal powers are defined in the documents that constitute the company. A company's basic capital is its share capital: the total capital is divided into 'shares' – legally defined units of ownership – that can be bought and sold on the stock market and that give certain legal powers of command to those who own them. Shareholders in a company have the right to stand for election to the board of directors, to nominate others for election, and to vote in these elections. They also have a range of financial rights to income and the right to attend, speak, and vote at company meetings.

In the simplest case, a single person may own all the shares of a company and, therefore, be able to exercise all the powers of command that are legally vested in it. However, the principal reason behind the introduction of the joint stock company is that the transferability of shares allows the capital available to an enterprise to expand beyond the personal wealth of any particular individual. The members of a family, for example, may join in the ownership of its shares, distributing them among themselves according to their contribution to its capital. The more extended is the family group, and the more wealthy are its individual members, the greater is the capital available to an enterprise. Where company shares can be bought and sold on a stock exchange, it is possible for companies to expand beyond the capital that can be supplied by any particular family. Shares can be sold, often in relatively small blocks, to individuals who are totally unconnected with the original family and are simply seeking an investment outlet for their capital. Shares can, therefore, be spread among a large mass of individuals who are unknown to each other. As modern capitalism has developed, certain types of company have themselves bought shares on the stock market. Insurance companies, investment companies, and banks have placed their funds in company shares in the hope of securing an income from dividends and, when they sell, a capital gain. Large companies, then, can be built up through the selling of shares to a large mass of individuals and to the growing numbers of corporate investors.

The fact that the capital of a joint stock company can be subscribed 'jointly' by a large number of individuals and other companies poses a fundamental problem of corporate governance. When a single owner is able to act as a sole director or can appoint compliant directors and managers, there is a unity of property ownership with the powers of command, or rule (Scott 1990b), within the enterprise. Where the single shareholder is a company rather than an individual, particular individuals (such as their own directors or managers) can be delegated to exercise these rights on their behalf. The dispersal of shares through a stock exchange, however, means that the vesting of the legal powers of command is no longer so straightforward. Voting power is crucial to shareholder power, and the number of votes held by a shareholder is, in general, directly proportional to the number of shares that they own. The overall distribution of votes, therefore, reflects the distribution of the shares. This means that when shares are dispersed among a large number of individuals and other companies, so too will be the votes. Ultimate legal authority in a business corporation is vested in a large, dispersed, and fragmented body of shareholders.

Various models of the relations between property ownership and the powers of command have been proposed to handle these complexities. The most influential of these has been that of the so-called managerialist writers, who took their lead from the pioneering work of Berle and Means (1932). They argue that the large corporation involves a separation of the financial interests of shareholders from their powers of command. Those who supply capital to a company and who, therefore, have a financial interest in its continuing success, may be so numerous and so diverse that they no longer have the power to determine the uses to which that capital is put (1932: 433ff). Berle and Means, therefore, distinguish the 'nominal ownership' of shares, which give financial rights, from the 'effective ownership' – or 'control' – that is involved in actually deciding how to use the corporate assets and employees. It was for this reason that they somewhat misleadingly described the modern corporate enterprise as involving a separation of ownership from control.

When there are very few shareholders, Berle and Means argued, control is directly linked to ownership, as the powers of command can be exercised by the shareholding group or delegated by them to others. As the number of shareholders becomes larger and more diverse, however, this is no longer the case. Decisions taken at company meetings and in elections are decided by a majority vote, and it is difficult to mobilise a cohesive majority block when shareholdings are highly dispersed. Each shareholder may have only a small proportion of the votes, and a very large number of share-holders must be brought together in a co-ordinated action if they are to shape the exercise of command. Berle and Means constructed a typology of modes of control that aimed to recognise the range of possibilities opened up by this corporate evolution.

Where there is ownership of a majority of the shares by a small and cohesive group, they speak of *majority control*. The majority shareholders can co-operate to exercise their legal rights to the full. As the controlling group gets larger, this co-operation becomes much more difficult to sustain. If, however, a cohesive group can still mobilise a substantial minority shareholding – and research has suggested that a holding of between 10 per cent and 50 per cent is sufficient – they may still have a 'working control' if the remainder of the shares are very widely dispersed. In this situation of *minority control*, the minority controllers are secure for so long as no countervailing group can mobilise against them.

When no group of owners can mobilise as much as 10 per cent of the shares, Berle and Means argued, proprietary control by majority or minority shareholders is no longer possible. In this situation of what they call *management control*, those who can legally determine the composition of the board of directors and who, therefore, have the ultimate powers of command are a large and anonymous mass of small share-holders who have no effective control. The ruling powers rest with those who actually succeed, through whatever means, in occupying key board and executive positions and who may be almost completely divorced from any legal ownership of the company's shares. Many managerialists have seen this management control as involving a usurpation of the ultimate powers of command by the internal, salaried managers who normally exercise only delegated command. Especially where they have technical and financial expertise, these managers may be able to fill the 'power vacuum' that exists at the top of the corporation. The board of directors becomes a self-recruiting management team that can run the corporation without having to face any significant influence from shareholders.

The idea of management control, however, has been heavily criticised. It has been pointed out that it assumes that the mass of shareholders is necessarily large, anonymous, and passive (Zeitlin 1989; Scott 1997). Even the smallest of individual shareholders tends to hold their shares only for so long as they continue to earn an income from them, and this imposes a fundamental constraint over management actions. Managers must, at the very least, ensure that they keep the enterprise in a profitable state. Where the shareholders are other companies rather than individuals, however, their power may be more active than passive. Corporate shareholders are both willing and able to pressurise the incumbent management and so may become a significant influence on the exercise of their powers of command. The nature of this causal influence will be discussed more fully in chapter 4, but it is important to recognise here that managerial command can rarely be separated to any significant extent from the structure of property ownership. Indeed, share ownership by companies has come to account for the great bulk of all share ownership, and the move to dispersal that was apparent in the data of Berle and Means long ago became a move back towards a relative concentration of shareholdings. As I will show, managerial command is significantly influenced by the shareholding interests of large financial enterprises, and the very term 'management control' may be inappropriate.

Within large business enterprises, however they are controlled, the powers of command are formally and legally concentrated within the board of directors. Crucial matters of corporate governance can always be investigated, therefore, through analyses of boards of directors and their relationship to the larger managerial hierarchy. Although there are legal variations in corporate form from one economy to another, it is generally possible to identify structural positions corresponding to the 'director' and the 'board' of directors (Scott 1997: 4–6). It is not unusual for directorships to be part-time positions and, therefore, for particular individuals to be recruited to two or more directorships in different companies. The acquisition of such 'multiple directorships' results in a network of 'interlocking directorships' into which individual companies are tied and that stretches across whole economies. Where command within a political system is focused on the central sovereign agency of its state, command within an economy is embedded in the more or less extensive structure of interlocking directorships that results from the recruitment practices of its many separate and competing sovereign enterprises.

Marxists have seen these networks of interlocking directorships as integral to systems of 'finance capital', in which large enterprises in all sectors of the economy are tied together and dominated by those who hold the multiple directorships (Hilferding 1910). These 'finance capitalists' form an 'inner circle' of corporate decision-makers whose life chances depend on their shareholdings and on income from these shares, and who constitute the leading edge of the capitalist class as a whole. Salaried managers, from this point of view, are merely the agents of the finance capitalists, exercising only delegated powers of command. They are part of a broad 'service class' (Renner 1953) that remains subordinate to the capitalist class. What is important is to recognise that the powers of command in a capitalist economy form an interlocking structure of top positions and that the exercise of command within individual enterprises cannot be seen separately from this.

C. Wright Mills pioneered the study of such intercorporate structures as necessary elements in any investigation of economic power. He noted the growth of the corporate sector of the US economy at the expense of personal, privately owned enterprises, and his 'corporate rich' included holders of substantial wealth (termed the 'very rich') along with those who held corporate office (the 'corporate executives'). He defined the 'corporate executives' rather loosely as the 'top two or three command posts in each of those hundred or so corporations which . . . are the largest' (Mills 1956: 126). By implication, this category includes most – but not all – of the multiple directors. However, Mills's definition highlights a central problem in positional studies of power: the problem of defining and demarcating the 'top' positions from those that seem to fall below them. When a state is being studied, it is usually possible to define the boundaries of the state elite, as the state forms a single territorial agency. In a corporate economy, however, the researcher must decide whether the 'top' corporations are, say, the largest 50, 100, 200, or 500, and what criterion is to be used to measure the size of them.

Mills himself saw the network of interlocking directorships as one component in the triangle of power that he called the 'power elite', which was formed from the interlocking and overlapping of the corporate rich, the political directorate, and the warlords. His approach to the corporate rich, however, has had an influence separate from this larger study. His analysis of the top corporate decision-makers as a corporate elite has served as a paradigm for much later work on economic elites. Mills was especially concerned with issues of social background in relation to what I have called 'class regimes of recruitment'. This approach has been especially important in analyses of economic power in large corporations, where researchers have examined the centralisation and dispersal of corporate power and the clustering of the powers of command into structurally distinct fields of activity (economic sectors) and business groups (see Mizruchi 1982; Scott and Griff 1984; Mintz and Schwartz 1985; Stokman et al. 1985; see also Scott 1991a).[9]

Research has consistently shown that holders of top corporate positions are recruited disproportionately from among the largest personal shareholders and their families, and that they enjoy the highest of earned incomes as well as substantial investment incomes. While directors typically hold very small percentages of the shares in their own companies (Scott 1997: 288, table 67), they have extensive portfolio investments across the whole of the corporate sector. By the end of the twentieth century, over a quarter of all large companies in Britain had stock option schemes that allowed their directors to build up shareholdings at discount prices and that could ensure them a dividend income up to six times as high as their salary. Directors and top executives in all the leading economies are now likely to have higher educational qualifications, rather than coming directly into business because of their family wealth, but they tend to have acquired their education at the private schools and top universities that are monopolised by the families of the wealthy and the privileged (Scott 1997: 292; Bourdieu and Passeron 1970). Allen (1978;

see also Allen 1987) showed that the rising trend in college graduation among multiple directors in the United States over the course of the twentieth century was associated with a continuing high level of recruitment from top private colleges, while Useem's (1984) study of Britain showed that the greater the number of directorships a man held, the more likely was he to have attended one of the major public schools. These class-based patterns of recruitment invariably coexist with gender regimes of recruitment. Only 5 per cent of directorships in the largest enterprises in Britain are held by women, and more than a half have no women directors at all.

3
Pressure and Policy Formation

States and other authoritarian organisations are not mere automatic emitters of decisions and commands. The decisions made by those in positions of authority are the outcome of processes of policy formulation and deliberation, and their outcomes are shaped by the processes of implementation and administration that follow. There is, then, a decision-making process that opens up possibilities for those who seek to influence the decisions that are made. This chapter looks at the processes of pressure through which this occurs. Pressure is counteraction by those groups that have a recognised place in the political systems that surround states and other sovereign organisations. The key means of pressure is persuasive influence through lobbying, negotiation, and discussion, but this is backed up by whatever inducements the pressure groups can mobilise: persuasion can be far more effective when associated with material inducements.

It has been pluralist writers who have most illuminated the mechanisms of pressure. Pluralist ideas can be traced back to at least the early years of the twentieth century, but they became particularly influential during the 1950s and 1960s. These arguments were largely developed as criticisms of elitist views of power, and pluralists sought to stress more diverse and dispersed forms of power (McLennan 1995). Pluralist arguments have been allied with a variety of theoretical approaches, but more recent statements of pluralist views of power have emerged from post-structuralism and post-modernism in the 1980s and 1990s (McLennan 1995).[1] Behind this theoretical diversity, however, is the shared view that power has to be seen in terms of the active and intentional exercise of power in a decision-making process.

For pluralists, it is pressure, and not command, that is the defining element in a political system and that is the key to understanding its decision-making processes. Some advocates of the pluralist perspective have gone even further, seeing no need to look beyond pressure to any other mechanisms of power: the pressure of one group on another is all that there is to the holding and exercising of power. I will show the strengths and the limitations of this argument, stressing the real achievements of pluralism in highlighting one particular aspect of power. I will argue, however, that even an analysis of this one aspect – pressure – has to be broadened by considering ideas raised by critics of pluralism.

Pressure and Polyarchy

Pluralists start out from the increasingly important part that has been played by companies, churches, and other associations in state decision-making since the late nineteenth century. While there were some important English examples of pluralist thought (Laski 1917, 1919; Cole 1920), it was mainly developed in the United States. At Chicago, Bentley (1908) drew on Simmel's work on group behaviour and the related ideas of the Chicago sociologists. Politically organised groups, Bentley argued, are generally recruited from larger social forces, such as classes and ethnic groups, and the contradictions among these social forces find their expression in group competition and conflict. There is, however, no one-to-one relationship between groups and social forces. For example, a class might be the basis for the formation of a large number of different groups, and any particular group may represent ethnic, religious, and other interests as well as class interests. Group formation always involves numerous 'splittings and consolidations' (Bentley 1908: 210) among social forces, resulting in an extensive cross-cutting of social influences.

Bentley's work had its main influence after the Second World War, when it was taken up by Lasswell and Kaplan (1950), Truman (1951), and Dahl (1957), who built contemporary pluralism as a critical response to what they denigrated as 'the stratification approach' to the study of power. They applied this label to those such as the Lynds (1929; 1937), Warner (1949), Hunter (1953), and Mills (1956), who, in their different ways, saw local and national power structures as reflections of class structures and who adopted broadly elitist views (see Polsby 1962). Though correctly making the point that some elite theorists overstated the importance of positions of command in the overall pattern of power, pluralists themselves tended to exaggerate the importance of group pressure and to minimise the partisan role of states. So much do pluralists ignore states that they hardly use the word at all: they refer instead to political communities, political systems, or polities as the arenas of power. Governments are seen simply as one type of agent among the many and varied groups that exert pressure on each other in political systems.

Power, in the pluralist view, is the ability to initiate alternatives that actually get to be adopted or to veto alternatives that are initiated by others. The study of power involves a focus on the securing of discrete and observable policy outcomes in specific decision-making processes. The basic unit of analysis is the individual actor, who is seen as having preferences and values that he or she seeks to promote in action. Groups such as interest groups and political parties are clusters of individuals whose preferences have been aggregated into collective choices. The preferences of these groups are mobilised through collective action and through the formation of alliances and coalitions, with the intention of influencing governments. Governments themselves are seen as neutral mechanisms for aggregating collective preferences and so producing policy outcomes (Arrow 1951; Buchanan and Tullock 1962; Buchanan 1975).

Pluralists hold that individuals have numerous different interests and are involved in many different groups. For this reason, groups tend to have overlapping memberships and any alliances that they form are unstable and shifting, their members pushing one way and then another in order to secure support. A political system is a diverse kaleidoscope of coalitions and competitive relations, with each political group having a different amount of influence in relation to each of the issues with which it is concerned (Held 1987: 189). In the words of one of the leading pluralist theorists, the system of government forms 'a protean complex of criss-crossing relationships that change in strength and direction with alterations in the power and standing of interests' (Truman 1951: 508).

Governments in modern states are recruited from political parties, but their policies are not direct translations of party programmes into political action. Pluralists have emphasised that elected governments are simply one element in the institutional framework through which policy outcomes are formulated and implemented. Alongside any government there is both a large array of public and semi-public agencies that have been empowered to regulate particular activities and a large body of private associations – the so-called 'pressure groups' – that attempt to influence the government.[2] Groups take whatever opportunities they have to pressurise political parties and other agencies to produce new policy decisions in their favour or to prevent them from abandoning policies that have already been enacted.

Dahl (1971) holds that the system of fluid and shifting pressures epitomises a democratic distribution of power, which he calls 'polyarchic democracy' or rule by multiple minorities.[3] The United States and other contemporary western societies, Dahl argues, have fragmented, dispersed power structures. They are 'fractured into a congeries of hundreds of small "special interest groups", with incompletely overlapping memberships, widely differing power bases, and a multitude of techniques for exercising influence on decisions salient to them' (Polsby 1960: 66). Such groups can help, through their pressure, to ensure that minority interests are not overlooked, and group pressure has been seen as an important safeguard against the electoral dictatorship of a majority over minorities. Political leaders in such a system act as the neutral arbiters of pressed demands, and not as autonomous political agents with their own agenda and interests. Political institutions constitute a market mechanism, an invisible hand that aggregates and reconciles political 'demands' with the 'supply' of policies. Through this competitive mechanism, conflicting interests are forged into a democratic equilibrium. The decentralisation and specialisation of political power ensures a democratic process of decision-making. This is not the classical liberal model of direct or representative democracy, but a novel, group-based model of democracy.

This pattern of pluralist democracy is seen as a characteristically modern political form that develops from premodern or traditional social forms and coexists globally with contemporary non-modern forms (Kerr et al. 1960; Inkeles and Smith 1974). Pressure politics, therefore, are seen as occurring to their fullest extent in stable and cohesive political communities. In order for pressure to be seen as a viable method for the promotion of political interests, individual and collective actors must see themselves as operating within an institutional framework that establishes the procedural ground rules for political action. This framework defines the legitimacy of a whole political order and is grounded in what Almond and Verba have called a 'civic culture' (Almond and Verba 1963; see also Putnam 1973) that establishes citizenship rights and the capacity for citizens to enjoy free political actions. A stable pattern of democratic representation, operating through the mechanisms of pressure politics, exists only if underpinned by these core civic values. In a civic culture, military action and violent counteraction are not seen as legitimate forms of political activity and, conversely, systems in which there is no consensus over civic values cannot easily confine political activity to the exercise of pressure (Eckstein 1961; Lipset 1963). Contention in such societies takes the form of protest rather than pressure. In a civic culture, governmental institutions provide the framework for a democratic political system that is responsive to the pressures exercised by individual voters and the organised groups of which they are members.

At the centre of attention for many political analysts have been political parties, which they see as central to interest aggregation and decision-making. Political parties are organisations that aggregate individual and sectional preferences into the programmes that they put forward in the hope of securing electoral support for their bids to enter government. Whether they form majority or minority governments, join coalitions, or remain in opposition, political parties are also a major focus for the pressure that other groups exercise on the governmental process. Campaign groups, interest groups, and voluntary associations of all kinds seek to influence governments by influencing political parties.

Pluralists have also explored the ways in which parties seek to build blocks of electoral support by constructing packages of popularly-supported policies around their core values or ideological positions. One strand of pluralist theory, however, has pointed to a supposed decline in ideological commitments during the second half of the twentieth century – rediscovered by postmodernists in the form of what Lyotard (1979) called 'the end of the grand narratives' – and has seen parties as becoming exclusively orientated by pragmatic strategies of vote maximisation (Bell 1961). On this basis, it is suggested that parties drift towards the centre of political opinion, ensuring that 'moderate' rather than 'extreme' demands are met.

The question of whether it is sensible to call a pluralist system 'democratic', without any reference to the wider aspects of power, need be of no concern here. What is important is the view of the political process that pluralists have proposed. They have stressed that, regardless of what we might be able to say about command and constraint, it is essential to consider the processes of pressure that exist in any society in which political groups are free to form and can be accorded a recognised role as legitimate members of a political system. They have, furthermore, suggested that pressure is a matter of power exercised in relation to specific issues and decisions on behalf of larger constituencies.

Decisions, Nondecisions, and Representation

The exercise of pressure through participation in decision-making has been studied principally in terms of the approach to power set out by Dahl (1957) and Polsby (1960; see also

Nagel 1975). Through highlighting the role of initiation and veto power in the actual process of decision-making, these studies have uncovered many important features of public policy-making and the politics of pressure. According to Dahl, as I showed in chapter 1, power is the observable effect that one person's behaviour has on that of another. Thus, Polsby argued that the powerful members of any society are those who 'initiate, modify, veto, or in some visible manner act so as to change outcomes' (1962: 95). One of Dahl's key contributions to political sociology was to point out that the power of an individual or group must always be seen as, in principle, specific in its scope. That is to say, pressure is exercised in relation to certain issues or areas of policy and it is often quite difficult to convert or transfer this power from one area to another. Dahl does not rule out the possibility that some individuals or groups may have power that is highly generalised across a society, but he refuses to follow some elitists in assuming this to be the case in advance. Any nominally identifiable elite, he argues, may consist of quite distinct and separate sections, each of which has power specific to its own particular domain of decision-making. Thus, he rejects an elitist starting point as likely to predetermine the results of an investigation. He prefers, instead, to focus on particular policy areas and the pressure exercised in relation to specific issues and decisions. Only when an actor's power has been studied in a number of such areas, may it be possible to draw conclusions about whether this power is, in fact, more general in scope.

Dahl and his followers have been criticised by those who share his concern to investigate actual processes of decision-making, but who feel that he gave a partial and one-sided view of this process. Principal among these critics are Bachrach and Baratz (1962), who have argued, as I showed in chapter 1, that Dahl concentrated only on one highly visible face of power that policy-makers present to the public. Bachrach and Baratz suggest that there is a second, hidden face of power that involves the back-door negotiations and deals that rarely come to public attention. This second face of power is the means through which certain issues and interests can be excluded from consideration by preventing them from entering the formal decision-making process.

Bachrach and Baratz see this exclusion of potential issues as occurring whenever some actors are able to take advantage of the values and social institutions that define the scope of legitimate political pressure. Power is exercised in decision-making, but 'Power is also exercised when A devotes his energies to creating or reinforcing social and political values and institutional practices that limit the scope of the political process to public consideration of only those issues which are comparatively innocuous to A' (1962: 87). An act that prevents a person or group from raising, considering, or deciding a particular issue is to be considered as an act of power, as the act of a principal in relation to a subaltern. Such an act of prevention may be tacit or overt, but it is not an act of 'decision-making' as this was defined by Dahl. It is not a decision not to act over an issue, nor is it a decision not to decide on it. It is an act that suppresses potential issues and ensures that they do not even enter the decision-making process. Bachrach and Baratz therefore describe this as an act of 'nondecision-making'.

Nondecision-making operates through the shared values and ideas that form the procedural 'rules of the game' under which decision-making takes place. These procedural norms comprise the institutional framework that regulates legitimate political action. Any such framework rests on certain values and assumptions and so is necessarily biased in the way that it operates. Institutional procedures 'operate systematically and consistently to the benefit of certain persons and groups at the expense of others' (Bachrach and Baratz 1970: 43). The bias favours the vested interests of the insiders and disfavours the interests of those who are excluded (Bachrach and Baratz 1963: 107).[4] Nondecision-making is action that creates, sustains, or mobilises this bias in order to suppress concerns or grievances that would otherwise be raised and considered in the decision-making process. While this may sometimes result from acts that are simply routine institutionalised practices and that are not intentional exercises of power, they can be as deliberate and calculative as any overt act of decision-making. Nondecision-makers may rely on existing social norms, or they may establish new ones that – intentionally or unintentionally – exclude issues and prevent matters from appearing on the political agenda.

Nondecision-making, then, involves creating or reinforcing barriers to the airing of issues about which there is concern or disagreement.

Bachrach and Baratz are, at one level, highlighting the well-known fact that political leaders are able to shape public opinion as well as to respond to it. The preferences and concerns of voters have been recognised, even by pluralists, as partly constituted by political parties, the mass media, and other agencies of cultural socialisation (Alford and Friedland 1985: 104). Public opinion is not simply the result of free and frank deliberation by an autonomous public: the 'demands' to which party politicians respond are partly produced by political activists themselves (Habermas 1962). Bachrach and Baratz go beyond this, however, and claim that there will also be deliberate acts of exclusion. Values or rules can be invoked, for example, to undermine the legitimacy of the claims or interests of a potential participant in decision-making. Because of their exclusion from decision-making that is relevant to their concerns and interests, the members of an excluded group become subalterns in a power relationship. They are unable to raise matters of concern to themselves and that they would like to see discussed in public policy forums. The expression of public opinion and public preferences may be 'systematically distorted' (Habermas 1970a and b).

Bachrach and Baratz cite the example of an educational policy domain in which there is a relative equality of power among participants in relation to the issue of public education (levels of provision in schools, examination successes, and so on). They suggest that this apparent equality can mask a great inequality of power between the wealthy and the rest of the population. Those who are wealthy, they hold, do not depend on public education, as they can afford to pay for a private education for their children. They have no direct stake in the issue of public education and are likely to leave decision-making about this to others. At the same time, however, they will wish to ensure that the issue of private education (tax benefits, recruitment policies, and so on) is 'organised out' of politics so that their educational privileges are not challenged. They may, for example, emphasise norms that define rights to freedom of choice and the obligation of the state to provide education for all who wish it. Private education is simply not a political issue, and those who would wish to raise questions about the relationship between, say, personal direct spending on private education and levels of public spending, through taxation, on public education, are prevented from doing so. Wealthy principals mobilise a bias that excludes private education from the political arena and prevents poorer subalterns from making it into a political issue (see also Lindblom 1977: 180).

Other contributors to this debate – most notably Lukes (1974) – have identified yet a further face of power. This third face comprises those processes of power through which interests are actually formulated. Where Bachrach and Baratz focused on the exclusion of consciously formulated interests, Lukes argues that it is possible that, in some cases, individuals may be subject to power without being aware of this: they may not even recognise that they have interests that need to be represented in the decision-making process. It is possible that those who are unaware of their interests may more easily act against them, even when they are acting from choice and in relation to explicit and clearly recognised preferences. That is, Lukes sees actors as motivated by their subjective interests, but as also having 'real interests' of which they may be unaware. 'Public opinion', then, may be mistaken.

Lukes exemplifies this through the work of Crenson (1971), who showed that people may have a real interest in avoiding industrial pollution that damages their health, though they may act in ways that run counter to this interest. They may, for example, wish to maintain the work and income opportunities that are generated by a particular industrial enterprise in their locality, but they may be unaware of the health risks that this poses. The presence of the industrial enterprise generates a 'real' interest in avoiding the kinds of industrial pollution that it produces, but local residents may be unaware of this. If they are unaware of their real interests, it is not even necessary for a principal to exclude them from decision-making – those who are unaware of their own interests will not even attempt to raise them for formal, public consideration. In such a situation, Lukes wishes to say, the controllers of the polluting enterprise are principals who exercise power over those subalterns who encounter the pollution in their daily lives but do not seek to raise it as a political issue. Location and employment policies that result in pollution – however unintentional – reflect exercises of pressure from which some are excluded and others exclude themselves.

Studies of pressure, then, have to be carried out by examining actual decisions in relation to particular issues: who is involved at each stage of the decision-making process, who is excluded, and whose wishes ultimately prevail. In the sphere of state decision-making this involves identifying the larger political system and exploring the pressures that are placed upon a government by those who are a part of this system. Domhoff has identified two distinct areas of interest-representation in which pressure operates. These are what he calls the 'special interest process' and the 'policy-formation process'. The special interest process comprises the means through which pressure can be used to promote the interests of specific organisations or sections of society with shared interests. This might involve the securing of tax advantages, changes in proposed legislation, or preferential administrative treatment. It may even involve the effective 'colonisation' of regulatory bodies by those that they are supposed to regulate. The policy-formation process, on the other hand, is the broader set of relations through which the exercise of pressure establishes society-wide policies concerned with substantive areas of decision-making. Pressure groups become involved in building a climate of opinion and a framework of decision-making rather than in securing favourable outcomes on specific issues. In practice, of course, the two processes are entwined closely with one another.

Central to the special interest process is the use of lobbyists and of financial incentives. Lobbying is the use by organised private interests of publicists, public relations consultants, lawyers, and others as intermediaries between themselves and state bodies such as legislative committees, regulating agencies, and executive bureaucracies. Lobbyists try, in particular, to cultivate and persuade those whom they expect to be favourably disposed towards the interests that they represent. They may, for example, target legislators who previously worked in their industry or area of interest – many lobbyists are themselves former employees of the agencies that they lobby. Committees and state bureaucracies seek expert advice, and effective lobbying organisations can present themselves as the possessors of relevant knowledge, even when this is self-serving advice. By providing information, they can shape the context in which decisions are made. They may even produce draft bills, amendments to bills, and other legal or financial documents that they can put in front of decision-makers along with more general information and advice.

Financial inducement is the other mechanism in the special interest process that Domhoff identified as a way in which associations can pressurise those that they seek to influence. This may involve such things as the provision of electoral funds and party office expenses or the provision of secretarial and travel services to hard-pressed legislators and administrators. This kind of pressure may easily shade over into direct financial inducement and political corruption. Even where direct corruption does not occur, so many state agencies are locked into a structure of lobbying that 'the process operates to the benefit of those who can afford expensive lawyers or who have direct access to government officials and their staff' (Domhoff 1979: 31).

Domhoff (1979: 31–7) showed the operation of the special interest process in the Pennsylvania insurance industry, where changes in the framework of regulation were proposed. Insurance companies lobbied heavily against this through their trade association and through direct contacts with ex-insurance industry employees in the regulator's office. They produced briefings and opinions, and they bought lunches and Christmas gifts for those they were trying to influence. They also lobbied the state legislature directly, aiming to draw in an additional, external source of pressure on the regulator. Not a single bill proposed by the regulator got through the legislature in the three-year period studied. In some cases, lobbying may go further and bring a whole agency onto the side of the lobbyists. Selznick (1949), for example, showed that a technocratic planning agency that sought to carry local opinion with it was successfully lobbied by local interests and became an opponent of the initial plan.

The policy-formation process is one step removed from the pursuit and promotion of specific interests, and involves participation in society-wide mechanisms of interest aggregation in relation to broad issue areas, such as economic, foreign, and welfare policy. The critical organisations here are large representative bodies for whole industries or sectors of society, the councils and committees associated with major business and governmental agencies, and various research institutes, think tanks, and foundations. Such groups operate through informal meetings and formal symposiums, briefings, working parties, and publications to persuade decision-makers of their views. They work especially well, Domhoff (1979) argues, when their pressure activities are reinforced by a shared social background of class, ethnicity, or gender that eases interaction in their lunch and dinner circuits, discussion groups, and formal meetings.

Domhoff sees these groups as promoting policies through consensus formation, alliance formation, and expertise formation. They provide settings for relatively informal discussions in which policy issues can be formulated well away from the glare of public attention, as they generally operate on an off-the-record basis. By bringing together business interests, other professional and associational interests, government leaders, and expert researchers, they allow the formulation of a consensus over policy issues, and they are the bases from which such ideas can be promoted through the mass media and the government. They also provide frameworks of negotiation and compromise in which support can be traded for participation in co-ordinated action. Interest-based alliances are formed through the exchanging of favours ('logrolling') that underpins the policy consensus, and these alliances structure the recruitment, training, and careers of those involved in policy-making. Finally, they create an aura of 'expertise' – discussed more fully in chapter 5 – that can enable them to claim to be acting in the 'national interest' rather than merely from partisan interests. This creates an aura of rationality, technocracy, and disinterestedness that can add moral force to their policy proposals.[5]

Networks of Pressure and Policy

The various mechanisms involved in the exercise of pressure have recently been brought together in discussions of policy networks.[6] The state or political system is seen as comprising a complex of arenas or domains in which power relations over specific types of issues can make themselves felt through the building of stable and enduring interorganisational relations. This framework has been spelled out by Laumann and Knoke, who argue that 'the appropriate unit of analysis for studies of policy formation is not the state understood in the institutional sense, but the state as a collection of policy arenas incorporating *both* governmental and private actors' (1989: 22). A policy domain relates to a particular branch of the state or an area of state activity, such as health, energy, education, industry, defence, housing, agriculture, and so on. It comprises a set of actors that are each oriented towards a particular policy area or set of issues and outcomes, and who may have to take one another's interests and actions into account. They have shared, but often conflicting, interests in the formulation, deliberation, implementation, and administration of policy in that area. The political system of a society comprises a whole series of nested and overlapping policy domains, with many agencies and organisations being involved in two or more of these.

Along with government departments and agencies (ministries, parliamentary or congressional committees, statutory bodies, etc.), policy domains include private actors such as trades unions, interest groups, business enterprises, and voluntary associations. Identifying the participants in policy domains is no easy matter, as their boundaries are not clearly or formally drawn. Nor are they abstract functional areas defined by the researcher. They emerge from the particular ways in which specific states have organised their activities and in which private groups have attempted to promote their interests. Researchers aim to identify the key actors – those whose views and actions 'count' – without ignoring those who are involved in nondecision-making. As Laumann and Knoke argue: 'Mere inaction . . . is an insufficient clue to marginality, since some consequential actors, without any overt action on their part, can have their interests taken into account through the reactions of other core members who anticipate their interests in particular policies' (1989: 24). Policy networks, then, are the patterns formed by the long-term alliances and enduring social relations that are built up by the actors operating within a policy domain as they seek to exercise their power (Rhodes 1981). They vary in their structure according to the particular relations that organisations establish with each other, and it has been suggested that policy networks can be ranged along a continuum from the 'issue network' to the 'policy community'. In an 'issue network', many interests are represented but only loose and shifting sub-groups are formed. In a policy community, on the other hand, a cluster of members with shared interests and a policy consensus are regularly involved in the making of policy and are able to exclude or control the entry of the more peripheral members of the policy domain (Hogwood 1987; Rhodes and Marsh 1992). Where an issue network is relatively 'open', a policy community embodies a specific relational bias that can be mobilised by its members to exclude or marginalise others within the domain.

Government agencies generally tend to encourage the formation of policy communities, especially where they want to ensure regular consultation and the smooth implementation of policy. There is no guarantee, however, that such a state-sponsored policy community will be either compliant or a conflict-reducing feature of the policy-making process. Indeed, a strong policy community may be able to capture effective control over sections of the state apparatus and involve them in its struggles against other state agencies and groups (Smith 1993). Whether state agencies predominate or not, the existence of a policy community generally allows a more consistent and coherent policy to be formulated and implemented than occurs with an issue network. Pressure from private interests may be strong and effective in the absence of a policy community, but it is likely to be less co-ordinated and directed.

Domhoff has shown that when policy communities are connected through the policy formation process into a broad range of policy domains, they acquire a wider societal significance and ensure a disproportionate representation of the interests of their members. The relatively fragmented issue network, on the other hand, comes closer to the pluralist image of dispersed centres of power. Any societal policy structure may, therefore, vary from the relatively closed form associated with the existence of a power elite and an extended policy community to the more fragmented form associated with issue networks and assumed in some forms of pluralist theory.

A further dimension of analysis is the extent to which any societal policy structure is given formal, public authority, transforming it from a network of pressure to an apparatus of command. This is the case in corporatist systems, where the members of particularly tight and state-sponsored congeries of policy communities are incorporated into the formal structure of decision-making by according them delegated powers of public command. It is, argues Schmitter,

> a system of interest representation in which the constitutive elements are organised into a limited number of singular, compulsory, non-competitive, hierarchically ordered and functionally differentiated categories, recognised or licensed (if not created) by the state and granted a deliberate representational monopoly within their respective categories in exchange for observing certain controls on their selection of leaders and articulation of demands and supports. (Schmitter 1979: 13)

The role of pressure within policy networks has been forcefully analysed in investigations into agricultural and industrial policy in Britain and the United States undertaken by Smith (1990; 1993). The agricultural policy domain in Britain works through ministerial policy committees, and the Ministry of Agriculture, Fisheries, and Food (MAFF) has to defend its particular proposals against the views of other Government departments (especially the Treasury). At the same time, it works in relation to the European Community and such private groups as the National Farmers' Union (NFU) and its counterparts in other European countries, the Country Landowners' Association, the National Union of Agricultural and Allied Workers, numerous food processing companies, and such specialised representative bodies as the

Poultry Farmers' Association. Environmental and consumer pressure groups may also be considered as involved in the policy domain.

There is a small agricultural policy community, whose core (MAFF and the NFU) is surrounded by a larger 'secondary community' of organisations that are consulted or involved on an irregular basis by the ministry (Smith 1993: chapter 5; 1990). The NFU aggregates and synthesises the demands of the various branches of farming and has good relations with other farm and landowning bodies, allowing the ministry to deal with a single farming point of view. Involving the NFU in such a close relationship with policy-making has effectively prevented farmers from making excessive or contentious demands. If they demand too much, going beyond the range of the acceptable, they risk exclusion from the influence that they have built up within the policy-making process. The limited involvement of those in the secondary community, and the effective exclusion from decision-making of many other domain members, has meant that agricultural policy can be presented as based on a consensus of informed opinion. Contentious matters are not formally raised and so do not appear on the MAFF policy agenda as challenges to its proposals, and agricultural policy does not appear as a contentious political issue.

While some have seen this policy community and the mobilisation of its bias as a sign of the strength of farmers and of their ability to capture a branch of the state for their own use (Self and Storing 1962; Wilson 1977), Smith has shown that the formation of the policy community was an initiative taken by the Government in the wake of a protracted agricultural depression in the late 1920s and early 1930s and in anticipation of war. This action institutionalised a policy agenda and institutional structure that effectively excluded groups with diverging points of view.

This alignment of power changed during the 1980s as new issues were forced onto the agenda from outside. Although the policy community had expanded to include more European bodies, other groups were still confined to the secondary community or were excluded altogether. Smith shows that problems with the Common Agricultural Policy created the opportunity for environmental and consumer pressure groups to push for consideration of new issues. The structure of policy-making and its institutional bias made it difficult for such issues to emerge from the routine channels of pressure politics. Greater concern for food safety issues and worries over genetically modified organisms, for example, have been forced onto the agenda thanks, in large part, to forms of protest that challenge what they see as the restrictive alignment of government with the farming interests within the existing policy network. The election in 1997 of a less responsive Labour Government, committed to the abolition of certain rural field sports and aiming to maintain high levels of fuel taxation, even for farmers, has meant that the policy community has been seriously weakened and no longer operates as it did in the past.

A US agricultural policy community was formed around the Department of Agriculture, Congressional agricultural committees, and farming organisations, with the State taking the initiative as it did in Britain. The American Farm Bureau Federation (AFBF), the leading farming association, however, was also involved in the day-to-day administration of agricultural and food price policies, and gradually increased its power relative to that of the Department of Agriculture and other farming organisations. The AFBF was, furthermore, closely linked to the Republican Party, while a rival organisation was linked to the Democrats. The agricultural policy community, then, was relatively weak and divided when compared with that in Britain, and it was difficult to secure any clear consensus over policy goals. The US agricultural policy community, therefore, became increasingly fragile during the 1960s and 1970s. Changes in farming, the declining economic significance of agriculture, and state fiscal problems led to a vast expansion in the number and type of groups involved in the policy domain. The policy community fragmented into something much closer to an issue network.

Industrial policy in Britain shows the great pressure exercised by business groups (Grant and Marsh 1977; Grant 1987). This pressure rests on the resources that groups such as the Confederation of British Industry (CBI) can obtain from their membership subscriptions, which allow them to employ a large professional staff, to lobby government, and to provide a stream of policy-relevant information to policy-makers. The CBI has been accepted by governments as the voice of business and it has generally had a close 'insider' relationship to policy. This has never, however, been a unified, single voice, and large companies have continued to exercise a separate influence over particular ministries and policy issues. Aerospace and engineering companies, oil and gas companies, and financial companies (Ingham 1984; Longstreth 1979), have all had close relations with different ministries. As a result, business pressure has been unfocused and uncoordinated, and it has not been possible to secure a stable, consensual, and enduring industrial policy (Smith 1993: chapter 6). The large policy domain operates as a sprawling issue network with, for the most part, only weak and short-lived alliances.

The US industrial policy domain has been organised around three key coalitions (Domhoff 1979). Each of these provides a setting for relatively informal discussions in which policy issues can be formulated away from the glare of publicity, and they are bases for more or less enduring negotiations, compromises, and alliances. They foster an image of expertise and of the ability to act in the 'national interest' rather than from partisan concerns.

The three coalitions are the 'Moderate Conservatives', the 'Ultra-Conservatives', and the 'Liberals'. The Moderate Conservatives are an alliance of the Council on Foreign Relations, the Committee for Economic Development, the Business Council, and many of the largest business enterprises. They have a key role in the centrist wings of both of the big political parties, and they have been particularly close to the executive arm of the state. Its members appear in many of the positions of command examined in elite studies. The Ultra-Conservatives include the National Association of Manufacturers, the Chambers of Commerce, the American Enterprise Institute, and many smaller enterprises. Their main links are with the legislative arm of the state, and they are linked closely to conservative Republicans and Southern Democrats. They were a major force in the rise of Reaganism and the establishment of a new Right political outlook. The Liberal alliance is much more loose-knit than the Conservative blocks. It is rooted in labour organisations and professional associations, and is linked to the liberal wing of the Democrats. It has no significant permanent link with any branch of the State, and has to try to secure its goals in association with the moderate Conservatives if it is to have any chance of influencing policy.

Domhoff shows that the Moderate Conservatives have been the predominant force in policy-making over a long period of American history. When they seek to secure political change, Moderate Conservatives can enlist the support of the Liberal alliance in an attempt to push this through. When they wish to block a proposed change, they can themselves keep it off the executive agenda and they can rely on the ultra-Conservatives to oppose its consideration in Congress (Domhoff 1979: 118).

4
Constraint and Hegemony

In chapter 2 I used Weber's account of authority to explore command in sovereign organisations. Weber contrasted this with what he called 'domination by virtue of a constellation of interests'. While command rests upon legitimacy, domination by virtue of a constellation of interests rests upon an expedient alignment of interests between a principal and a subaltern. The participants have differing resources and they make rational, calculative choices about how to protect or enhance those resources and the opportunities that they generate. The manipulation of facilities and their use as sanctions allows people to offer and accept inducements to act in desired ways. Weber found the clearest examples of what he had in mind in the power relations that result from competitive exchange relations in markets. He held that a person who monopolises resources that are in demand has the potential to act as a principal in a power relationship (Weber 1914: 943). The monopolist is able to influence the conduct of others by setting the conditions under which they can gain access to the desired resources and by restricting the range of options that others consider to be relevant to their intended actions. This form of domination, then, rests on mechanisms of coercion and inducement that *constrain* action alternatives. In a relation of constraint, a principal can control the actions of subalterns without the need for any explicit direction or any expression of his or her wishes. Subalterns can respond to an anticipated reaction.

The most characteristic form of this kind of constraint, according to Weber, is where a large bank, because of its control over vast financial resources, has the ability to influence the behaviour of companies seeking capital for investment and expansion. Such a bank can set conditions for access to loans and working capital. These reflect the bank's calculation of where its own financial interests lie, and other enterprises are left with the freedom to choose whether or not to accept these conditions. These conditions may include not simply the immediate financial costs of credit but also, for example, management changes and legal or financial reorganisations. In so far as enterprises choose to meet the conditions necessary to obtain the desired credit, they become subalterns in a power relationship.

This constraint must be distinguished from both command and pressure. Constraint, as I use the word here, occurs wherever control over resources and opportunities allows some agents to set the conditions under which others must act. Principals are systematically advantaged (and subalterns are systematically disadvantaged) by virtue of the capacity that principals have for the actual exercise of power. Because they have this capacity, however, they may not need to issue orders or exercise pressure on a routine basis. Whether intentionally or not, subaltern agents act under manipulated conditions of action and they must take account of the inducements that are offered and the anticipated reactions of their principals. To constrain is to severely restrict or limit the options that are available to rational calculators, bringing about a mutual adjustment or concordance of interests. Subalterns concur in actions that accord with the wishes or interests of a constraining principal because it is in their own interest to do so. Constraint is leadership by restriction: the possessors of superior resources restrict the autonomy of others by limiting the range of relevant considerations and, therefore, the courses of action that they feel are feasible and desirable.

Financial Power and Economic Constraint

Economic constraint rests on the possession of or control over goods, skills, and capital. Economic agents adopt strategies that are aimed at enhancing their control – and therefore their autonomy – in the economic conditions under which they must act. The 'resource dependence' (Pfeffer 1981) of one enterprise upon another, therefore, is the basis of the power relation between them. Constraint usually operates in close relationship with the exercise of pressure. Principals who cannot secure their interests through constraint are likely to become more interventionist and to pressure their subalterns into conformity. This relationship between pressure and constraint in the economic sphere has been central to ongoing debates over managers and managerial power in large enterprises.

Debate around the managerialist theory of corporate power has highlighted the importance of legal property relations for the exercise of command within business enterprises. The transformation of property relations since the beginning of the twentieth century has made the growth of managerial authority appear to be the most important feature of corporate governance. What I showed in chapter 2, however, was the considerable evidence that there is for the continuing importance of property ownership in relations of corporate command. Whether on a majority or a minority basis, share ownership remains a crucial means of access to positions of command in big business. In many large enterprises, however, shareholdings have become so dispersed that no single shareholder can exercise even minority control. It is this trend that seems to offer support for the claims of managerialist writers that non-propertied agents can usurp the powers of command that formally belong to the shareholders.

It is a growth in shareholdings by corporations and financial intermediaries, and a corresponding decline in the proportion of shares that are owned by individuals and families, that has eliminated personal shareholder control from many large enterprises. When shares are spread widely among a large number of holders, the board of directors can exercise its decision-making powers unconstrained by the presence of an owning controller on the board. Far from leading to 'management control', however, the trend in corporate ownership has meant that managerial autonomy is now constrained by the dominant shareholding institutions. This is because shares in large enterprises are not totally dispersed among a fragmented and anonymous mass of passive shareholders. They are held by a relatively small group of banks, insurance companies, pension funds, and other financial intermediaries who actively pursue their interests on the stock market and through the credit system. This situation has been described, developing Weber's ideas, as one of 'control through a constellation of interests' (Scott 1997: 48ff).

In a large business enterprise the biggest shareholders – typically around twenty of them – form a constellation of financial interests that together have sufficient shares to exercise a real and effective constraint over corporate decision-making, though they do not generally exercise direct command. The big shareholders in an enterprise are not direct personal associates of each other, they have few joint interests, and they are divided from one another by their competition in the financial markets. For all these reasons, there is little basis for them to co-operate over the long-term towards the attainment of positions of command in particular enterprises. The principal shareholders, then, have effective possession, but they have little unity or capacity for collective action. Each financial shareholder pursues its own sectional interests, and their shared interests are – by and large – limited to their common concern for the financial success of the company in which they jointly invest. Each big shareholder invests in many enterprises, facing the same situation in each of them, and so is unable to spend more than a small proportion of its time on the affairs of any one enterprise.

Despite this absence of shareholder command, however, the boards of directors cannot simply disregard the interests of their big shareholders. They depend upon them for their future capital needs, and they will need their support when they want to be re-elected as directors or to have their business policies endorsed at an annual general meeting. The constellations of shareholding institutions therefore exercise a continuing constraint over managerial decision-making. Institutions that are dissatisfied with the performance of the companies in which they invest are able to sell all or some of their shares on the market, and this is often the most cost-effective way of securing their own financial interests. The sale of large numbers of shares by their largest shareholders, however, is something that most enterprises will seek to avoid: it puts a pressure on the share price and makes it more difficult for an enterprise to satisfy its remaining share-holders and to meet its future capital requirements. Share sales are especially worrying when a company is fighting a take-over bid (Chandler 1990: 740). In order to forestall the possibility of large-scale share sales and to help them to build support for their policies, managers try to ensure that they know and can meet the financial expectations of their major shareholders: managers anticipate the reactions of their large shareholders.

The big shareholding institutions, then, set the broad financial conditions under which managers must act. In for-mulating their decisions, managers must take account of the balance of shareholdings and the interweaving of interests among the shareholders that are the members of their con-trolling constellation (Zeitlin 1974). The control situation in most large enterprises is not one of management control, as depicted by Berle and Means (1932), but of control through a constellation of interests or, as Herman (1981) calls it, 'constrained management control'.

This situation is quite different from domination through command. A shareholder representative who sits on the board of directors of another enterprise has a legitimate right to participate in its decision-making and to contribute to the issuing of orders in its name. Institutional shareholders without board positions have no such right to issue orders. They constrain from outside and without any deliberate or overt intervention in decision-making. Their control over financial resources allows them to determine the broad con-ditions under which other enterprises must make their own business decisions.

Shareholding institutions – like other economic stake-holders in an enterprise – can also pressure managers to act in one way or another. As I have suggested, this is a relatively costly option and is unlikely to be used if constraint proves effective. In some situations, however, pressure becomes a necessity. When the market price of a company's shares is already low, or when an institution holds such a large block of shares that no likely buyer can be found, a dissatisfied institution will have little alternative but to try to secure its interests through more direct measures. It will hold behind-the-scenes meetings with the company's managers, it will request more detailed financial information, and it may demand changes in management or in corporate strategy. Where a number of institutions feel similarly dissatisfied – and it is likely that most informed and active investing institutions will have a similar view – there will be very strong pressure on the internal management of the failing enterprise. Without the need for any formal alliance, financial institutions may push for the implementation of similar policies, leading to the appearance – from the outside – of formal co-ordination. Most typically, however, this is focused but non-cooperative pressure, with the lead being taken by a small subset of the controlling constellation.

Constraint and pressure, therefore, are complementary means of power in corporate affairs. Those with the powers of command are subject to the constraining power of big shareholders, and when these routine mechanisms of constraint prove insufficient the shareholders resort to short-term pressure aimed at restoring a situation in which they can, once again, rely on constraint. Thus, Glasberg (1989) has shown that bank conceptions of 'normality' and 'crisis' structure their willingness to invest or intervene in the affairs of a company that seeks capital.

Control through a constellation of interests is now widely found in Britain, the United States, Australia, and Canada, where their particular structures of banking and credit have encouraged the growth of large financial intermediaries. This pattern of control has established itself most strongly in the United States, where it is found in almost two thirds of the top enterprises. In Britain, where both family ownership and ownership by foreign multinationals has remained strong, it accounts for just under a half of all large enterprises, and in Australia it accounts for just over a third. In

Canada, where the level of foreign ownership is especially high, the figure drops to just under one in ten of large companies (Scott 1997: Tables 12, 17, 23, and 24). Related forms of depersonalised constraining control are found in France, Germany, and Japan. Here, however, shareholding relations tend to be tighter and more long-term, allowing constraint to be combined with some direct participation in corporate command. In Japan's 'alliance capitalism' (Gerlach 1992), for example, enterprises are formed into large and cohesive business groups within which the chief executives of the leading enterprises collectively exercise command over their group.

In addition to these processes of constraint at the level of individual enterprises, institutional and corporate ownership has resulted in the building of larger structures of financial constraint at the level of the national economy. When many big financial institutions hold blocks of shares in large numbers of enterprises, businesses of all kinds come to be tied together through interweaving institutional shareholdings into a network of capital relations. These structures were first glimpsed by Hilferding (1910) in his analysis of the development of finance capital, though he saw this as tending towards a centralisation of the powers of command in the hands of bank directors. In fact, contemporary forms of finance capital more typically operate through a structure of constraint rather than command. Although large shareholding institutions have central positions in these networks, constraining the decision-making powers of many subaltern enterprises, they rarely act as centres of command. Indeed, these institutions are controlled in precisely the same way as the enterprises in which they invest – by other institutions – and the network of constraint is organised around a circularity of power relations, with very few absolutely sovereign centres of command.

While financial institutions generally seek to avoid a close and continuing involvement in the affairs of particular enterprises, their directors are willing to take seats on a limited number of other company boards and the directors of other companies may be invited to sit on bank and insurance boards. As a result – albeit unintentionally – a network of interlocking directorships is built alongside the network of shareholdings. In the Anglo-American economies, there is no one-to-one association between shareholdings and directorships and, therefore, there is only a limited association between constraint and command. Banks and other institutions that lie in central positions in the intercorporate networks are not agents of corporate command, but they do exercise a considerable influence over the flow of capital and the flow of information about the availability of capital and investment opportunities. In addition to their control over capital, then, the big financial institutions are nerve-centres in the communication networks that connect large enterprises. Their centrality in these flows means that they shape the knowledge and information that subaltern decision-makers rely on in formulating their corporate policies.

Finance capital, then, is a structure of collective financial constraint:

> Numerous large financial interests hold powerful positions within the business world, but they do not exercise direct control over particular dependent enterprises. Their collective control over the availability of capital, however, gives them the power to determine the broad conditions under which other enterprises must decide their corporate strategies. Those enterprises that are involved in the provision of credit through the granting of loans and the purchasing of shares are those in which is institutionalised the collective power to constrain corporate decision-making. (Scott 1997: 139)[1]

Roy has described this simply as 'structural power', which he defines as 'the ability to determine the context within which decisions are made by affecting the consequences of one alternative over another' (1997: 13). Structurally powerful agents set the choices that others face and determine the consequences of their making these choices. At the turn of the twentieth century, Roy shows, the owners of many moderately-sized manufacturing enterprises chose to amalgamate with one another and to incorporate – so diluting their controlling holdings – rather than continuing to act independently. They did this because of the strong market position of the largest manufacturers and the importance of their financial backers to this monopoly power. A small unincorporated enterprise faced the stark choice between competing against a large monopoly that controlled the salient resources or becoming a part of the monopoly. As Roy concludes, 'If they lacked the power to beat them, their decision to join must be explained in terms of the corporations' power' (1997: 260). Similarly, Mintz and Schwartz (1985; 1986) have documented the bank constraint that today organises corporate decision-making in the United States, allowing them to structure the framework in which business activity takes place.

Economic constraint is not, of course, confined to national economies, and it is becoming increasingly difficult to conceptualise national economies independently of the global economic structures in which they are embedded. Constraint is an integral feature of the expanding transnational economic relations, but these are, however, closely entwined with transnational political relations. They are most usefully seen in terms of the formation and restructuring of global political economies.

Political Constraint and Hegemony

I showed in chapter 2 that contemporary states are sovereign organisations of coercion and command. They are strategic actors that systematically, and often aggressively, pursue their national interests and that seek to maximise their power relative to other states. In the absence of overarching global structures of command, relations between states are determined by their ability to mobilise force and their possession of scarce economic resources. The consequences of this for diplomacy, trade, and warfare have been explored by the so-called 'realist' writers on international relations, such as Morgenthau (1948), Kaplan (1957), Schelling (1960), and Waltz (1979). According to these writers, whatever may be the internal powers of command that are available to a state, its power in relation to other states is a matter of the distribution of resources between them and the constraint

that each is able to exercise. In normal circumstances, therefore, the sheer existence of military force – and the implicit or
anticipated threat of its use – may give states a powerful position of constraint within the international system of states.
Similarly, control over financial resources that are central to
the international flow of investment and production can allow
states and transnational enterprises to influence the actions of
other states and their member organisations by shaping the
economic conditions under which they must act.

International agencies do, of course, exist, and they have
varying degrees of authority in relation to their member
states. Realists argue, however, that there is a constant
tension between inter-state constraint and transnational
command. This has been seen in terms of a distinction
between 'hierarchy' and 'anarchy'.[2] Inter-state relations,
according to this point of view, are 'anarchic' in the same
sense that competitive market relations are anarchic. They are
the outcome of strategic calculation and the exercise of constraint, unregulated by any secure framework of legitimacy.
They must be understood, in the same way as markets, as
patterns of rational choice based on coercion and inducement. It is within such 'anarchic' structures that internally
'hierarchical' states operate, and command relations are
most typically limited to the intra-state level. In some circumstances, it may be possible for inter-state relations to be
formed into supra-national authoritative bodies. In most
cases, however, such hierarchical structures are difficult to
establish: anarchical relations of constraint prevail and a
more or less unequal balance of power exists.

This realist emphasis on strategic power politics is
altogether too rigid for a comprehensive understanding of
inter-state relations, and the main challenge to the realist
approach has come from those who have highlighted the
growth of international political and economic relations and
of inter-state organisations. In stressing the need to theorise
non-state agencies and transnational relations, many of
these critics have drawn on pluralist ideas to examine the
exercise of pressure at the international level (Keohane and
Nye 1971). More radical critics (Bull 1977) have sought to
explore the ways in which the relations of states to non-
state agencies can form systems of action with distinctively

new social institutions of global governance (concerning, for example, human rights, minimum welfare standards, and environmental protection) that limit, to a degree, the exercise of national self-interest.

Inter-state relations have increasingly involved the setting up of new transnational agencies, such as the International Monetary Fund (IMF), the World Bank, the United Nations, the North Atlantic Treaty Organization (NATO), and the European Union, that have themselves become the objects of diplomacy and strategic negotiation. As well as these international agencies there has been a growth in the importance of interstate economic relations. These are the transactions of private, non-state agencies, mainly business enterprises, located within the territorial boundaries of one or another state. These are often referred to as non-governmental organisations (NGOs) in order to also include regulatory bodies and other non-commercial agencies.

International arrangements of various kinds often reflect the dominance of one or another state, but they can also have a legitimacy and institutional reality of their own. They may constitute what Keohane (1984: 8) calls 'international regimes': systems of rules, norms, principles, procedures, and forms of organisation that supplement the structures of hierarchy and constraint in inter-state relations. Examples of international regimes would be the post-Second World War regime of international payments and trade, the nuclear non-proliferation regime, the regime of universal human rights, and the emerging regime of ecological protection. International regimes revolve around particular values or principles in relation to their specific tasks or problems, but they coexist and overlap one another, and they vary quite considerably in both their strength and their extent. They are not mere coercive structures with repressive powers, but are normative structures embedded in transnational frameworks of command that go some way towards countering the absolute sovereignty of nation states.

Like all institutional frameworks, international regimes can be analysed in terms of the processes of pressure that they make possible and, in consequence, the processes of nondecision-making and bias mobilisation that they allow. Theories of constraint in international relations go beyond this recognition of pressure and the institutional bias of transnational social institutions to look at the structural power that constitutes dynamic inter-state systems and that generates a global differentiation between principal and subaltern states. Principal states are the 'core' members of a world system. Subaltern states, on the other hand, are those that are confined to the 'periphery'. Peripheral states become subalterns in this system of power because their trading patterns and development strategies are shaped by their location within market, production, and investment relations that are organised around the interests and resources of the core states.

The development of these ideas owes a great deal to the framework of world systems analysis, associated in particular with the work of Wallerstein (1974; 1980; 1989; see also Hopkins and Wallerstein 1982). This sees inter-societal systems as fields of political and economic competition among nation states, business enterprises, and those who command them, together with various international and transnational agencies. A world system is an inter-societal system that is integrated through a network of trading transactions and a common division of labour, but is divided into a large number of separate and competing political, cultural, and other territorial units. It is a single economic system that is fragmented into territories ruled by separate sovereign states. The formation of monopolies, coalitions, and alliances among the members of a world system builds patterns of constraint that constitute certain states as the 'core' states of the system, the states that are able to determine the conditions under which 'peripheral' states must act.

The modern world system developed as a Europe-centred system between the fifteenth and sixteenth centuries, and its core states have, until recently, been exclusively European states or states of European settlement. The early core states of England, France, and the Netherlands dominated a periphery of fragmented states that related to one another through diplomacy and warfare. As the world economy came to embrace ever larger parts of the globe and to adopt industrial technologies of production, the core expanded and its membership shifted. Increasing levels of economic concentration within the constituent national economies during the course of the twentieth century resulted in a growing importance within the core of the United States and, later, Japan.

International regimes reflect the underlying balance of power between core and peripheral states, and a particularly important question in international relations theory has been the extent to which one or more of the core powers can be considered as a 'hegemonic' state (Kennedy 1987). The word hegemony is now better known from the specific definition that Gramsci (1926–37) gave to it, and I will look at his ideas later in the chapter, but his work drew on existing ideas from the study of national and international politics. It is this core meaning that is important here. Hegemony is a word with Greek origins, having been used to describe a structure of power in which one of the ancient Greek city states was able to take a leading position with respect to the other city states with which it coexisted and co-operated. The term referred, therefore, to leadership exercised by one member of a confederation or association: a hegemonic state is the most influential member of a group or system of states. Hegemony, then, refers to the supremacy of one state or a small set of states over other, formally independent states. The term cannot be used, for example, to refer to the imperial power of a colonial state within its empire, as imperial systems are organised around clear patterns of authoritarian, hierarchical command. The states in a system of hegemony retain their formal freedom of decision and action, though they are *de facto* constrained to act as if they were subject to explicit commands. As Susan Strange has argued about constraint in international relations: 'What is common to all kinds of structural power is that the possessor is able to change the range of choices open to others without apparently putting pressure directly on them to take one decision or to make one choice rather than others' (Strange 1988: 29, cited in Brown 1997: 179).

At its most basic, hegemony rests upon a preponderance in the distribution of material resources – of raw materials, capital, and both economic and military technology. This economic and military preponderance, the basis of coercion and inducement, is at the heart of inter-state constraint. The greater the concentration of these powers of constraint, the more restricted are the purely anarchic tendencies of an inter-state system and the more likely are transnational social institutions to be built. To this *de facto* constraining power, then, may be added the ability and willingness of the hegemonic state, or states, to maintain the institutions that comprise an international regime. A hegemonic state, in the strongest sense, has the ability and willingness to make and to enforce transnational rules, and the peripheral and other states are able and willing to acknowledge this role. Where hegemony goes beyond mere constraint, then, is in the existence of a degree of *consent*: 'Hegemony rests on the subjective awareness by elites in secondary states that they are benefiting, as well as on the willingness of the hegemon itself to sacrifice tangible short-term benefits for intangible long-term gains' (Keohane 1984: 45). While its ultimate basis may, indeed, be constraint, it also involves long-term consent and not mere *ad hoc*, case-by-case submission. This element of consent was what Gramsci emphasised in his discussion of hegemony, which he saw as introducing a particular cultural or ideological element to power. Where constraint is sheer *de facto* structural power, hegemony involves a degree of *de jure* normative consent. It falls short, however, of the hierarchical relations of command that were discussed in chapter 2.

The periods of relative peace and stability that were ensured by British supremacy in the eighteenth and nineteenth centuries, and by American supremacy in the second half of the twentieth century – the periods often referred to, respectively, as the *Pax Britannica* and the *Pax Americana* – have often been cited as examples of international hegemony. Keohane (1984) claims that such periods of stability and order can only occur when there is a single hegemonic power – there can only ever be one hegemon, at most, in any inter-state system. However, it is not at all clear that this should be the case, and there is no reason why there may not be a *polyarchic hegemony*, or condominium, of a small set of states. Just as it is possible to see the polyarchic constraint of a set of banks in a system of finance capital, so there can be polyarchic constraint and polyarchic hegemony in inter-state systems. The work of Chase-Dunn and his colleagues suggested that the modern world system shows an oscillation between periods in which a single core state has hegemony and periods in which there is a more or less equal distribution of power among a group of core states. Where there is no single hegemon, they argue, there is a greater likelihood of warfare among the core states: the absence of a sole 'superpower' weakens the military stability on which a more or less secure peace depends (Chase-Dunn and Podobnik 1999).

The importance of recognising a distinction between single-power hegemony and polyarchic constraint is apparent from trends in global power since the Second World War. The period from roughly 1947 to the early 1970s was marked by a gradual build-up of US hegemony in international relations.[3] The military power of the United States provided a basis for the use of its economic resources in building a specific international regime of political economy. The key institutions of this international regime were an international monetary system centred on the IMF and the World Bank, a programme of tariff reduction embodied in the General Agreement on Tariffs and Trade (GATT), and a system of cheap oil for Europe and Japan based on American influence in the Middle East.

Together with the domestic Keynesian policies that were pursued by the leading states, this cluster of institutions ensured a stable and secure period of economic growth under US leadership. The implicit or explicit threat to mobilise economic and military resources in support of its interests helped to ensure that weaker states anticipated American interests. Because of such anticipatory reactions, the United States had only occasionally to state its preferences openly or to intervene formally in the affairs of other states. American agencies did not control 'simply by commanding their weaker partners' but 'had to search for material interests with their partners' (Keohane 1984: 138): 'America was not able simply to dictate terms to the world, but it had multiple ways of providing incentives to others to conform to its preferences' (1984: 177).

Economic and military constraint was conjoined with an ideological opposition to Communism that provided a basis through which European states consented to US leadership. Although inducement and coercion, rather than command, were the key factors, US dominance was embodied in transnational institutions that other states accepted, that they regarded as legitimate, and that would, therefore, eliminate any need to rely completely on rewards and punishments.

From the early 1970s, however, the United States could no longer be regarded, without qualification, as the hegemonic global power. The European Community, which was at first a support for US hegemony, became an increasingly important independent focus of power, and the oil crisis destroyed the support previously gained from cheap oil. The weakening power of the hegemon and the rise of other powers to challenge it required the US to resort, increasingly, to coercion and inducement. Although the collapse of the Soviet Union enhanced US military power relative to that of other states, its economic power could no longer match its military power. The international regime was reconstructed on a multilateral basis that reflected a more evenly balanced distribution of constraining power between the United States, Germany, and Japan. Although Germany predominated in European affairs, it was far from exercising exclusive hegemony either on a European or a wider basis. Similarly, Japanese predominance among the Pacific Rim economies, was increasingly challenged by other economies and, most notably, by the rise of China.

The world system has, therefore, come to be marked by multilateral, polyarchic constraint rather than by US hegemony. Transnational institutions are now sustained 'because they can facilitate agreements and decentralized enforcement of agreements among governments' (Keohane 1984: 244). They are rooted in and reinforce polyarchic constraint. Alliance-building among the core powers leads to the formation of extensive transnational political networks and new transnational agencies with varying powers of command. Such trends open up opportunities for the use of the positional methodologies discussed in chapter 3 to investigate the possible formation of transnational elites, and for researchers to explore the exercise of pressure at a global level.

State Power and Class Hegemony

Chapter 2 was concerned with the structure of positions within state systems and the patterns of recruitment to these positions. I showed that, for many Marxists, closed patterns of recruitment to concentrated structures of command was the crucial basis for inferring the existence of a ruling class. For other Marxists, however, the power of a dominant class is manifest not so much in command as in constraint and hegemony. This argument has significantly enlarged the debate over state power, pointing beyond command and the exercise of pressure to the structures of constraint that surround state institutions.

The most forceful advocate of this restriction in the scope of elitist and pluralist arguments has been Poulantzas (1969; and see Poulantzas 1968). In his critical review of Miliband's (1969) argument, Poulantzas held that states are the overall regulating and co-ordinating mechanisms within societies but are not the mere 'instruments' of particular social groups. State power, he argued, has a class character in so far as it advances and promotes the interests of a dominant class, and this occurs wherever a state's activities sustain the conditions necessary for the continued reproduction of that class and its relations to other classes. This does not depend on who does or does not occupy the top positions in a state apparatus; it is, rather, a matter of how a state actually responds to the constraints that it faces in making its decisions. This rejection of positional studies did not lead Poulantzas to advance a pluralist methodology, however. Where pluralists have seen states as neutral arenas in which groups exercise pressure, Poulantzas saw them as arenas of class power. They are channels through which class power is realised. In a capitalist society, he held, a state can do *nothing other* than promote the interests of a capitalist class, no matter who may occupy the top positions of command.

Poulantzas took a particularly strong line on this issue, holding that command and pressure are purely contingent consequences of the objective alignment of class interests that constrains a state to act in one way rather than another. He was unclear, however, about the specific mechanisms through which this constraint operates. Later work, and particularly that of O'Connor (1973), has filled this gap and has been more willing to recognise that the constraint mechanisms operate alongside command and pressure mechanisms in the overall pattern of state power.[4]

O'Connor's starting point is the fiscal mechanism through which states are dependent on the satisfactory performance of their economies (Schumpeter 1954). As I showed in chapter 2, any state must raise the finance that it requires to meet its own running costs. It must have a system of taxation to raise revenue, and the flow of tax income will depend on the ability of its economy to generate a large enough surplus. Tax revenue can be sustained or increased only when the economy is thriving, and in a period of economic contraction it is likely to have to reduce the level of its expenditure. Tax income can be supplemented, to a certain extent, by borrowing or by following Keynesian budgetary principles, but the possibilities offered by these, too, are ultimately dependent on economic performance. A state, then, must promote the economic basis on which its own revenue depends.

The effects of this mechanism in a modern society are amplified by the State's need to secure the support and consent of its citizens. These citizens expect that their standard of living will be maintained or improved, and they come to judge their state by its ability to secure the conditions that make this possible. If economic conditions deteriorate, there is likely to be a particularly high demand for welfare spending and for improvements in opportunities for earnings and employment, but this is precisely the time at which it is most difficult for a state to maintain its tax revenue. When a state cannot meet the demands of its citizens, they are likely to withdraw their support for the Government and other state agencies. A government that does not wish to see its support crumble is, therefore, constrained to ensure that state expenditure is geared towards maintaining or improving private economic performance. States in capitalist societies, argues O'Connor, face constantly increasing demands for state expenditure on the infrastructure that supports private production as well as on health, education, and welfare. There is an inherent structural gap between state revenues and state expenditure, a chronic 'fiscal crisis' that constrains state policies.

The constraints identified by Poulantzas and O'Connor are the result of a complex structure of relations that is produced through the actions of business enterprises and consumers but is not reducible to them. The investment and employment decisions of individual business enterprises (operating in markets structured by financial and political constraints) have their effects on state policies principally through their macroeconomic consequences. While states can, and do, respond to pressures from individual enterprises – as I showed in chapter 3 – they also respond to the constraints that are imposed by the macroeconomic processes on which they depend. It is the overall level of investment and employment in an economy, for example, that matters to a state. Business enterprises and consumers act in such a way as to alter the macroeconomic framework in which a state must operate if it is to secure its revenue. Anticipating these changes, states tend to act in ways that will protect or promote business interests.

Integral to Poulantzas's account of state power is his reliance on Gramsci's (1926–37) concept of class hegemony. The subordination of a state apparatus to the constraints of capitalist production is seen as one element in the overall hegemony exercised by a dominant class. Gramsci developed his concept of hegemony in explicit opposition to orthodox Marxist views that reduced class power to economic constraint alone. He recognised that, in addition to economic power, a ruling class held powers of command within state apparatuses and that their political power was not a mere reflex of economic power. Most crucially, however, he sought to recognise the importance of the organisation of ideological discourses into forms of cultural power that were essential conditions of class rule. Taking his lead from writings on international power, he extended the concept of hegemony to include not only the political and economic dominance of a class but also its cultural dominance (Bates 1975). Gramsci argued that class power involves both the economic and the political dominance of a class through its powers of constraint and command and the exercise of 'intellectual and moral leadership' (Gramsci 1926–37: 57). This cultural leadership involves precisely the mixture of constraint and consent that is central to the use of the concept of hegemony in international relations (Abercrombie et al. 1979: 12; Anderson 1976).

Economic constraint, political force, and authoritative command are central to the power of a dominant class, Gramsci argued, but this dominance is most strongly secured when cultural representations constrain the alternatives that people consider and lead them to consent to their own subordination. Consent, according to Gramsci, is engineered or manufactured, albeit unintentionally. It is produced through specific techniques and practices of control that are located primarily in 'civil society', in the social sphere outside of the state. Churches, factories, trades unions, schools, and other social organisations and locales are the places within which consent is generated through the formulation of ideas and the socialisation of individuals. Similarly, state apparatuses are not merely coercive apparatuses, and Gramsci recognised that political organisation can also be a means through which ideas are developed and inculcated in individuals (see also Poulantzas 1968; Althusser 1971).

What Marx called 'the ruling ideas' of a society are those embodied in its principal social organisations and institutions. They become the taken-for-granted world view of its members and are generally unquestioned: they simply reflect the way the world works. As Mann (1970) has argued, popular acceptance of prevailing ideas generally rests on an attitude of 'pragmatic acceptance'. Cultural constraint operates through the routinised and taken-for-granted solidity of everyday life: 'It is a powerful, constraining environment that appears entirely natural to social actors' (Abercrombie et al. 1979: 166). Subalterns comply with the anticipated preferences of principals because they see no meaningful alternative definition of the situation. Learned cultural significations shape the ways in which people see the world and can lead them to consent to forms of leadership that may work against their own interests. This consent may come close to a system of command if a pragmatic acceptance becomes 'normative acceptance'. This is likely to occur when subalterns internalise the values of their principals and treat their wishes as legitimate orders.

Applying these ideas, Parkin (1967) has argued that schools and the mass media in Britain tend to inculcate a set of broadly conservative values that are congruent with those embodied in its principal economic and political institutions and that shape the attitudes and actions of all members of British society. Miliband (1969; 1982) has also explored the content and substance of these values and tied this to an investigation of positions of command in mass-media organisations. His work, like that of Domhoff (1979) in the United States, showed that command and constraint operate jointly, through the ownership and control of the mass media, in the conversion of class hegemony into ideological domination.

This is not to imply that individuals are completely without choice, that they are perfectly socialised cultural dopes. Gramsci emphasised both the diversity of socialising institutions, seeing them as operating in more or less contradictory ways, and the fact that individuals reflect upon their own diverse experiences and are able, to a greater or lesser extent, to formulate an autonomous understanding of their own situation (1926–37: 419). Subalterns, therefore, possess the capacity to resist, even if they generally consent to the leadership of their principals. For Gramsci, the key to this resistance was to be found in the mass political party and the intellectuals who helped to develop a practical political consciousness among its members. Parkin's work (1967; see also Parkin 1971) emphasised the ways in which the Labour Party in Britain was sustained by the institutions of local working-class communities, and how each of these was the basis for the development of radical oppositional ideas that ran counter to the values embodied in the dominant social institutions. The hegemony of a ruling class, then, can be opposed by a 'counter-hegemony' constructed in subaltern social institutions and life experiences, a possibility that will be examined more closely in chapter 6.

5
Discipline and Expertise

The central figure in the second-stream view of power today is, undoubtedly, Michel Foucault, who has stressed that any form of power, other than mere force and physical repression, depends on the formation of individuals into subjects with appropriate motives and desires. Through processes of signification, Foucault argued, individuals become socialised members of groups and are interpellated – incorporated – into power relations. Their power or lack of power derives, quite literally, from their empowerment or disempowerment by the groups of which they are members. Foucault's particular contribution was to explore these issues in relation to those processes of social control that he called 'discipline'. There is a repressive aspect to discipline, but there is also a more important 'productive' side through which individuals are formed as subjects. Foucault saw this as increasingly occurring under the aegis of 'experts', whose empowerment is due to their formation by scientific and technical forms of discourse. In modern societies, expertise had become a central element in the disciplining of populations. Experts are empowered as principals by virtue of the recognition of their legitimate competence to intervene in ways that produce disciplined – and even self-disciplined – subalterns.

Expertise, then, is central to the dynamics of power in modern societies. In pre-modern societies, most people were able to avoid having any significant daily contact with priests and other claimants to expert knowledge (Giddens 1991: 30). Modern societies, however, have experienced a massive expansion in systems of technical and scientific knowledge and in the numbers of experts who are involved in these systems. Experts today are all but unavoidable. Non-experts are convinced or persuaded to accept the claims that are made by the experts because of 'expert systems' – systems in which technical knowledge is acquired through long and specialised training – that encourage the building of *trust* on the part of the lay majority in the expert minority. In this chapter, I will look at the relationship between discipline and expertise, and I will also look at how this new viewpoint extends earlier work on the nature of 'professional' power in contemporary societies.

Government, Discourse, and Discipline

Foucault did not integrate his voluminous writings into a single and systematic theoretical statement, making it difficult to summarise his general ideas in a clear and consistent form. Indeed, he consistently refused to provide definitions of his key concepts, and many of his most important ideas have been expressed differently in his various works – sometimes even in the same work. In addition to this, Foucault did not read at all widely in the literature on power that he, nevertheless, felt able to reject as inadequate.[1] Despite this, he does provide a compelling and powerful argument that adds a great deal to our understanding of power.

Foucault saw the modern period as marked by the establishment of a particular form of domination that he called *government* (Foucault 1978). This term refers not simply to the body of ministers of state and the political means through which they work, but to a whole complex set of processes through which human behaviour is systematically controlled in ever wider areas of social life. Government takes place both within and beyond the state apparatus. It comprises systems of authoritarian control that combine two aspects of power: sovereign powers of command and productive, disciplinary powers. The system of sovereign powers of command, analysed in chapter 2, comprises the 'juridical' or 'repressive' forms of power. They are the coercive structures of exclusion, repression, and punishment from which the processes of government begin but which are not its whole. Sovereign power leaves subalterns as autonomous agents, but subjects them to external controls and inducements. Government is also a practice through which, under the umbrella of repressive power, disciplinary power forms individuals with the motives, desires, and orientations that enable them to act as properly-formed members of the governed social groups. Though resting on physical punishments or mortifications, discipline most particularly involves forms of mental and physical 'training': the very subjectivity of subalterns is constituted through mechanisms of power. Disciplined individuals have acquired skills, habits of action, desires, and qualities of character that allow them to act in appropriate and expected ways and to do so through the exercise of self-control (Hindess 1996: 113). Modern rulers have come to see their task as one of government in this sense of the shaping, guiding, and directing of the conduct of others by using persuasive processes of signification and legitimation to work through their desires, aspirations, interests, and beliefs (Dean 1999: 11).

Modern states – as Weber showed – are concerned with ensuring their sovereignty over their particular territories *vis-à-vis* other states and international agencies. Sovereignty over a territory also involves the management of its population through regulating the life processes through which they live, work, and relate to each other. This is what Foucault (1976) called 'bio-politics', a term that he uses very widely to refer to controls over the biological conditions of birth, health, illness, sex, and death, and over the cultural and environmental conditions that shape human biology. Disciplinary power, in the form of bio-politics, is that specific aspect of modern systems of government that is concerned with controlling individual human bodies and, therefore, the agents whose bodies they are. There is, Foucault claimed, an 'anatomo-politics' of the human body itself at the heart of modern regimes of government.

In its most general meaning, discipline is the control that is exercised over people through systems of rules that are not simply imposed on them but are instilled in them. This emerged first in the ascetic discipline of the medieval monasteries and was later established in a range of Church organisations, such as poorhouses and orphanages. It is this sense that Foucault draws upon and extends, holding that such discipline is established in more and more areas of life as bio-politics becomes all-pervasive. Modern disciplinary power developed as the cumulative consequence of many small changes scattered around a whole array of locales: in colleges and primary schools, hospitals, military barracks, workshops, and so on. Innovatory ideas and practices circulated more or less rapidly from one locale to another, until the cumulative effect was 'a blueprint of a general method' of discipline (Foucault 1975: 138; Clegg 1989: 168–73). Central to this blueprint was the idea of the body as an object of power, as something that can be subjected, used, transformed, and improved through 'dressage', through regimented training, and through exercise. The 'docile body' (Foucault 1975: 136) that results has capacities to act in specific required ways, and these capacities are exercised voluntarily as a result of training and the self-monitoring of thoughts and actions.

What is central to Foucault's argument is that modern discipline arose as an aspect of the building of systems of expertise. A whole complex of scientific disciplines and other discursive formations established the systems of ideas through which disciplinary bio-politics could be exercised to govern populations.[2] The various bodies of specialist, technical knowledge that proliferated with the growth of modern government – economics, law, accounting, medicine, psychiatry, criminology, and so on – all contributed, in their contradictory ways, to the building of the system of discipline. Each has defined the particular categories of the population to which their specific forms of discipline are appropriate. For example, criminology conceptualised criminals, social administration the poor, and psychiatry the mentally ill as the objects of their respective discourses and forms of discipline. Together they inform the organisations and practices through which these groups are governed.

The expert application of discipline, Foucault argued, required the establishment of specific structures and mechanisms that make possible the training and shaping of bodily habits. Disciplinary structures, he argued, are 'carceral' organisations that confine people in tightly defined places in order to operate on their bodies.[3] Carceral organisations rest on a system of 'disciplinary coercion', or external regulation, over the actions of their members. This control is made effective through systems of surveillance that Foucault called the institutionalised 'gaze'. This supervisory system allows experts and officials to observe, judge, and examine the behaviour of the inmates in routine and systematic ways (see Savage 1998; Dandecker 1990).

These organisations also involve a disciplining of the body through the structuring of *space*, *movement*, *exercise*, and *tactics*. The space in which disciplinary power is exercised tends to be 'cellular' in its organisation. That is to say, it forms an enclosed space within which individuals and categories of individuals can be partitioned into physically separate sub-spaces and assigned distinct tasks according to their category or status, as defined in the governing discourse. Movement around this enclosed space is controlled through timetables, programmes of 'drill', and other schemes for the articulation of body, gesture, and objects. These controls over movement ensure that participants follow a highly structured rhythm in their lives, encouraging them to develop corresponding physical habits and routines of action. Foucault used the term 'exercise' to refer to the ways in which timed schedules of activity are organised into planned sets of goals or targets that are subject to regular examination. Graduation, promotion, cure, and release, for example, are set up as goals whose achievement – as assessed through practices of diagnosis or accreditation – leads the governing experts to assign appropriate identities to the subalterns. Finally, Foucault highlights the tactical structuring of space through the concerted articulation of people into teams or co-ordinated groups whose members can respond automatically to appropriate signals of command.[4] 'Panoptic' mechanisms of hierarchical observation that allow comprehensive and close supervision, together with the use of internal enquiries, tribunals, and systems of penalties, underpin the central importance attached to the examinations through which accreditation takes place. Medical examinations, school examinations, and similar mechanisms of assessment transform individuals into documented 'cases' with their particular place in the archives of written documents that Weber saw as central to modern bureaucratic administration.

Foucault saw the prison as the central and most important type of carceral organisation to emerge in modern European societies. Prisons stood at the centres of extensive networks of carceral organisations. They were connected, for example, to orphanages and psychiatric hospitals, that, in turn, stretched out to connect with charitable societies and 'improvement' associations, lodging houses, and workers' estates. These interlinked agencies, networked through their overlapping forms of discourse, formed what Foucault (1975: 301) called a 'carceral archipelago': a network of expert power through which disciplinary controls reached throughout the entire society.

Though he did not develop the idea himself, Foucault's argument points to the way in which a carceral archipelago coexists and intersects with other disciplinary networks in a society. Medico-psychiatric archipelagos, educational archipelagos, and manufacturing archipelagos, for example, join with the carceral archipelagos in the overall disciplinary regimes of government in modern societies. These networks of discipline divide social space into more or less distinct fields of activity: criminal justice systems, welfare systems, health systems, educational systems, and so on. Each such sphere of action is organised around its characteristic forms of discipline, reflecting the particular forms of discourse that lie behind them. Though they interpenetrate, overlap, and colonise each other, they are – to a greater or lesser extent – separate and distinct, each with its own autonomy relative to the others. The overall system of government in a society is not a co-ordinated and integrated totality, but a dispersed and fragmented assembly of diverse 'disciplinary projects' (Hindess 1996: 118).

These ideas are clear from Foucault's earliest works on the birth of the mental asylum (1961) and the teaching hospital (1963). At the same time that prisons emerged as the central carceral organisations, so teaching hospitals emerged as the foci of new practices involving the clinical investigation and treatment of bodily disorders. The medical faculties of the universities and the organisation of the medical profession established a new focus on the sick body, rather than simply on clusters of disease symptoms. Diagnosis and treatment were rationally and systematically pursued as a 'scientific' project of investigation into lesions and disorders, drawing on evidence derived from the dissection of dead bodies. The end of the eighteenth century also saw the development of a new discourse of insanity that structured the asylum and regimes for the 'treatment' of mental problems. 'Retreats' from mainstream society were set up as locales where expert treatment of the insane could take place under conditions of confinement. These asylums were also closely linked with the emerging organisation of clinical medicine, medical personnel being brought in as the embodiment of the 'scientific' treatment of the mind. There was, Foucault argued, a medicalisation of madness.

It was in his discussion of the treatment of those who were defined as insane that Foucault first intimated a feature of discipline that took on a greater importance for him towards the end of his life. The treatment regimes of mental asylums, he argued, were built around an assumption that mad people needed to gain an insight into their own condition and an awareness of their moral responsibilities for their own actions (1961: 246–7). With the development of psychoanalysis and related therapies, patients were brought into a dialogue with their doctors, participating in the 'powers of language' inherent in the 'talking cure' to bring about this insight (1961: 250). Thus, bodies were confined and disciplined in order that a reflexive self-awareness could be encouraged and an alteration in minds could be achieved. External discipline was the basis of self-discipline.

Foucault's work on the external, imposed discipline of regimentation, classification, and surveillance, is, to a great extent, an extension and enlargement of Weber's view of modern authority and administration. His later work on the internal self-discipline that the external techniques of discipline attempt to produce, however, was a major theoretical innovation. By the time that he wrote the final volumes of his *History of Sexuality* (1984a and b), Foucault was far more concerned with this second aspect of disciplinary power, and his focus was on the interiorisation of the disciplinary gaze and its employment in practices of self-surveillance by reflexive agents. This transformation of external discipline into internal discipline is the main achievement of the experts whose forms of discourse organise the locales and define their non-expert members as subalterns. Through the inculcation of practices of self-reflection and self-control in those with whom the experts deal, expert practitioners become the principals in patterns of what Foucault called 'confessional' or 'pastoral' power. This involves practices of spiritual guidance, moral confession, self-disclosure, personal example, and discipleship.[5]

In modern societies, then, a whole array of systems of discursive knowledge come to be concerned with the constitution of human beings as 'subjects', as free but disciplined agents. Practitioners of pastoral power draw on these forms of discourse in an attempt to persuade their subjects to participate in their own subjection. They attempt, for example, to bring criminals to an awareness of the need to 'reform' themselves, and the mentally ill to a realisation of the need to be 'cured'. Such practices of pastoral power are central to the expertise of the counsellor, the therapist, the social worker, the personnel manager, and others in the caring and curing professions as they work to inculcate the 'techniques of the self' on which modern regimes of government increasingly depend.

Expertise and Professionalism

Foucault's discussion of the discursive formation of disciplines shows how an analysis of authoritarian command and coercive forms of power can be linked to the emergence of particular forms of expertise. Specialised branches of state activity, such as the provision of health, education, and welfare, come to require the employment of experts for the delivery of their services. In these agencies, it is often experts who hold positions of ultimate authority, their power combining command with expertise. Thus, a doctor is an expert in relation to his or her patients, but may be both an expert and a holder of a position of command in relation to the nurses and technicians who work alongside him or her in a hospital or clinic. Similarly, many business enterprises rely on experts for undertaking some of their activities: they employ accountants, lawyers, industrial chemists, engineers, and so on. Not only do these experts play a key role in the provision of services to business customers, they also undertake technical roles within enterprises and they participate in the wider structure of managerial command.

Foucault's concern was with those forms of expertise that give rise to discipline, but not all expertise is of this type. The growth of scientific discourses has resulted not only in expertise in relation to people but also in the appearance of numerous forms of expertise in relation to objects such as the physical environment, buildings, and machines of all kinds. Their character as expertise is, however, similar to that involved in disciplinary power, and many of these forms of expertise have become increasingly entwined in disciplinary archipelagos. Surprisingly, however, Foucault gave relatively little attention to the nature of this expert power. His recognition of the interdependence of command and expertise, nevertheless, provides a basis on which earlier writings on expertise can be reformulated. Despite Foucault's apparent rejection of all prior approaches to power, the study of command and expertise have a long history in sociology and Foucault has, quite independently, rediscovered many of the insights established in this earlier research on the nature of the 'professions' and their powers over their clients and customers.

Contemporary understandings of the professions have their origins in Parsons' development of the ideas of Durkheim (1939; 1940; see also Durkheim 1917). Although many aspects of his approach have been criticised, his basic point of view remains an essential starting point. Parsons defined professional occupations as those that temper the purely instrumental orientations of managerial and commercial occupations with a 'service' orientation rooted in their specialist knowledge. Thus, the word 'professional' does not refer to the intrinsic features of particular occupations, but to a specific way in which some occupational roles have come to be organised. A successful claim to professional status is possible whenever those in an occupation can plausibly claim to possess a distinct body of specialised knowledge that is essential for the exercise of their occupational tasks. The key resource that underpins their power is their control over a body of knowledge and skill that has not been appropriated by others (Freidson 1993: 40). Their knowledge-claims are organised through discursively formed symbolic monopolies that organise the systems of licensing, regulation, examining, and other forms of exclusionary closure that professionals employ to buttress their position. With the establishment of this kind of professional organisation, the knowledge and skills of an occupation can be acquired only through a process of training or apprenticeship that is controlled by the established members of the profession themselves (Freidson 1970a; Johnson 1972).

Professions, then, have institutionalised expertise as the basis of their power. Expertise differs from command in the nature of the discursive formation involved in the power relationship. Parsons argued that whereas administrative power in bureaucracies is organised as a rational, legal form of authority through impersonal legal procedures, professions are founded in the impersonality of scientific knowledge. Professionalism is a form of occupational control that exists because of a monopolisation of abstract knowledge and the practical techniques that are based on it. Specialists in medicine, law, education, welfare, management, and social work, for example, are those 'whose powers are based on their professional training and their possession of esoteric ways of understanding and acting upon conduct grounded in codes of knowledge and claims to special wisdom' (Rose 1998: 12; see also Larson 1977). The basis of a professional practice is a system of abstract knowledge that is sustained through academic work of classification, investigation, and instruction, and that is embodied in forms of diagnosis and treatment. The experts themselves are the producers and transformers of this knowledge, and they generally partici-pate in the exercise of the practical techniques. Much of this practical work, however, may be delegated to other workers who are subject to the control of the professionals (Abbott 1988: 8–9). Expertise, then, involves power relations with other professions and with subordinate assistants, as well as with clients.

A discursive monopoly is a 'cultural machinery of jurisdiction' (Abbott 1988: 59): it allows practitioners to assert and legitimate their 'jurisdictional claims' over certain problems and matters that are potential objects of action and further research for them.[6] As Freidson argues, however, 'Knowledge itself does not give special power: only *exclusive* knowledge gives power to its possessors' (Freidson 1973: 67). A jurisdictional claim is operative only when it is publicly recognised in exclusive rights in relation to practice, payment, entry, promotion, accreditation, and so on. Experts establish professional jurisdictions in their struggles against others for rights over a particular sphere of activity. In establishing exclusivity and closure, they define themselves not only in relation to their clients but also in relation to other professionals. Professional occupations, therefore, come to be connected into expert divisions of labour – extensive social networks of interconnected tasks – and expert jurisdictions that form the backbone of the disciplinary archipelagos of modern societies (Abbott 1988: 86). Professional claims are particularly strong when they are underwritten by state power, and when expert rights can be legally enshrined and protected through the authority of state agencies (Freidson 1970b: 83).

Parsons himself did not explore the power dimension of professional organisation to any great extent, but he did highlight a problem in Weber's account of administrative power. Specifically, he held that Weber did not properly distinguish between hierarchical authority and expertise (Parsons and Henderson 1947: 59). Hierarchical authority is the authority of office, where influence is a function of the position occupied. Expertise, on the other hand, is the authority of competence and involves an exercise of persuasion based on a common universe of discourse among colleagues and a knowledge-gap between experts and the lay people who depend upon its use (Freidson 1970b: 109; Rueschemeyer 1983: 41). The full implications of Parsons' argument, however, were drawn out by Gouldner in his own critique of Weber's typology of administration (Gouldner 1954a; see also Gouldner 1954b).

Gouldner held that Weber's account of bureaucracy did not look properly at the processes through which administrative rules are initiated and made effective. In some systems, Gouldner argued, administrative rules are established through a process of 'imposition', and these are the rules that lie behind relations of command.[7] In such a situation, the obedience of subalterns has to be seen as an end in itself that expresses their consent to the authority of the principals, regardless of the rationality or the morality of any particular order. Principals are seen as having a right to impose whatever rules they choose, and to back them up with coercion or rewards whenever necessary. In other situations, however, rules are established through 'agreement' among the participants, and Gouldner sees this as characteristic of those systems in which principals claim and are accorded expertise. Subalterns recognise the technical character of expert knowledge and see its use as something that will benefit them or will produce outcomes of which they approve. Obedience, then, is a means to an end: subalterns are persuaded that it is the best way of achieving a goal that they desire.

On the basis of this discussion of obedience, Gouldner suggests a typology of bureaucracies. In a *punishment-centred bureaucracy* – the kind on which Weber focused his attention – administration involves the enforcement of commands in the face of potential conflict and 'grievance' actions by subordinates. In a *representative bureaucracy*, on the other hand, officials have a relevant technical competence and training; subordinates see definite (though perhaps only potential) advantages flowing from their application of the rules. They value the rules because they value the outcomes, and there is likely to be only a very low level of resistance to particular commands (Gouldner 1954a: 193). Officials are likely to help to build this kind of support through processes of 'education': subalterns must be socialised or disciplined into an acceptance of expert power.[8] This is, in Etzioni's (1961) terms, a form of 'normative power', operating through persuasion, suggestion, and commitment, and Gouldner characterises it as what he calls a 'proto-democratic' authority (1954a: 221).[9]

This kind of representative power extends beyond the formal limits of a bureaucracy to affect those who come into contact with experts in a whole variety of situations. The power of a doctor over a patient, for example, reflects the patient's acceptance of or agreement to the knowledge that underpins the technical claims to expertise that the doctor makes. Power through expertise and 'education' is all-pervasive in societies that place a high premium on technical knowledge.

Gouldner combined two ideas that ought perhaps to be distinguished. There is, first, the *claim* that principals make to technical knowledge and expertise, and there is, secondly, the *acceptance* of these claims by subalterns. Claims that are not accepted may, nevertheless, be established by imposition and punishment – through the mechanisms that Foucault was later to call 'coercive discipline'. Expertise exists only when both of these elements coincide. Inmates in a concentration camp, for example, do not 'agree' to the use of the medical knowledge of the doctors who experiment on them, even though they may recognise that they do have a technical competence. When expertise claims are, however, accepted – not always in quite the 'voluntary' way that Gouldner suggests – they become the basis of the very different form of productive power that was stressed by Foucault.

This model of administration, then, sees knowledge-based competence defining people as experts – or, strictly, as in occupations characterised by expertise. Those who make use of expert services do not have the knowledge to solve their problems for themselves. Patients, for example, cannot effectively cure themselves – or do not routinely feel that they are able to do so – and litigants cannot easily represent themselves in legal actions. Acceptance of professional competence, then, disempowers patients, litigants, and other users of expert services, making them the subalterns of the professional participants.

This involves the building of trust, which Gouldner has seen as one of the central institutional features of modernity. People acquiesce in the exercise of expert power when they place their trust in the body of knowledge and the competence of the practitioner to define the risks that they face and the actions necessary to treat them (Giddens 1989: 84). Trust is not built from an informed acceptance of the evidential basis for the body of knowledge – the knowledge-gap precludes this – but involves simply a practical acceptance of expert knowledge claims on the part of those who have no rational grounds for appraising them. People are de-skilled or unskilled in many areas of modern life, and they place their trust in those who they believe have the knowledge and skills to cope with the problems that they encounter. Where such trust is not established, expert services are not controlled through professionalism and will be controlled, instead, by individual or corporate patrons or by state agencies (Johnson 1972). In this situation, experts are drawn into structures of authoritarian command. They may be mere subordinates in such structures, or they may have delegated authority that allows them to exercise their expertise. Accountants, in corporate economies, for example, have generally exercised their expertise as an integral part of the complex managerial hierarchies of large business enterprises. Their exercise of expertise and the establishment of an element of representative bureaucracy operate alongside of and subordinate to the exercise of command within a punishment-centred bureaucratic system.

This contrast between 'professionalised' and 'bureaucratised' expertise has defined a long-standing tradition of research (W. R. Scott 1966). Experts organised as professionals have high autonomy in their work situations. They are involved in collegial relations of control over their work and conditions of employment, and they are strongly oriented towards the wider profession and the knowledge that they promote and apply in practising their expertise. They have strong horizontal orientations and connections to other members of the same profession: in Gouldner's (1957) terminology, they have a strong 'cosmopolitan' orientation. Experts who are not self-employed professionals, but are the employees of large bureaucratic organisations, have less autonomy in their work and employment relations. While doctors and lawyers have often been able to practice in small firms on a self-employed basis, 'engineers, professors, clergymen, and scientists must work in and for organisations' (Freidson 1993: 41). Subordinated to hierarchical structures of command, they tend to have strong vertical orientations and connections to others within the same organisation: their position involves what Gouldner called a 'local' orientation.

Many occupations fall between these two extremes. Where employing organisations are specialised around the provision of expert services, for example, the experts working within them may retain some basis for a professionalised form of occupational control. The nature of the expert work is defined and regulated outside the particular organisations in which it is delivered – through professional associations and through regulatory and training bodies, or by the professionalised workers themselves (as in universities and teaching hospitals). This is the case, for example, with most law firms, accountancy firms, hospitals, social work agencies, schools, and universities. The central expert task is performed and controlled by professionalised workers who have a degree of autonomous regulation over their own conditions of work; and where professional work is supervised and controlled this is generally done by other trained experts (Freidson 1973: 64). Line management, then, is concerned principally with securing and maintaining the financial, clerical, and other supportive work that is necessary for the delivery of the expert service. Thus, 'A hierarchical structure of authority is often found, but it is professional not administrative, based on the authority of imputed expertise rather than on the authority of administrative office. . . . An administrative structure does exist, but it is restricted largely to authority over supportive economic, clerical, and maintenance services' (1973: 65).

Many experts employed in bureaucracies, however, are locked into a structure of legal or procedural administration in which their expertise is subordinated to commercial or state considerations and in which, therefore, they are directly supervised and monitored by superior authorities. They may be organised into a line-staff organisation, or they may become an integral part of the line administration itself (Freidson 1993: 38). Such bureaucratised experts are likely to experience strains and conflicts because of the contradiction between their claims to competence and their subordination to command relations. Their claims to autonomous expertise and power are undermined by their subaltern positions in larger structures of command. Many such experts are, at best, 'semi-professionals' (Etzioni 1964; 1969). Social workers and nurses, for example, have been widely seen in this way, as semi-professionalised expert staff whose autonomy is increasingly limited by the superior power of both senior administrators and the more fully professionalised doctors. This bureaucratisation of expertise has been especially marked where gendered patterns of recruitment exist and where, therefore, female semi-professionals become subordinated to male line managers and professionals (Gamarnikow 1978; Witz 1992). Such conflicts lie behind struggles over professionalisation strategies aimed at raising the level of training and credentialism involved in such work. The development of nursing degrees, for example, may be supported by nurses as a way of enhancing their professional expertise, but the nature and content of these degrees are rarely determined by nurses themselves.

It is often argued that there is a long-term 'deprofessionalisation' or 'proletarianisation' of expertise (Oppenheimer 1973; Esland 1980). The development of information and communications technology and the general expansion of education, it is argued, has reduced the knowledge-gap between experts and lay people. Diversification of knowledge leads to competing groups of experts, lay access to knowledge has been enhanced, and the willingness of lay people to trust any particular group of experts has been weakened. As a result, the monopolisation of knowledge is less marked than it was in earlier stages of modernity and there is a weaker basis for the jurisdictional claims made by experts. At the same time, a growing scale of production, increasing dependence on competitive markets, and a growing tendency to regulation undermine the autonomy of experts in their workplaces. Many service organisations in which expertise has been organised professionally have become increasingly bureaucratised in this way.

These processes, however, are not inexorable, and the extent of any deprofessionalisation will be quite variable from one occupation to another and over time. Where the conditions do apply, the bureaucratised expertise increases at the expense of professionalised expertise. The growth of accountancy firms in an economy dominated by multinational enterprises, for example, has locked them ever more into the kinds of corporate structures for which they provide their services, and public-sector hospitals have been put under funding regimes that require them to become more 'business-like' and to tie senior medical and nursing staff into line-management careers. In such circumstances, line management expands and expert autonomy in relation to their own work declines. Teachers in schools and lecturers in universities, for example, face inspection visits, teaching and research assessments, and a range of other bureaucratic tasks that strengthen line management *vis-à-vis* experts and turn more and more of them into part-time or full-time managers. If they remain as principals in power relations, this owes more to their holding of positions of command than it does to their expertise.

For many writers, this has fundamental implications for sovereign power. Expert knowledge plays an ever-greater role in policy making as decisions come to be seen as technical matters rather than issues for contentious discussion. For Habermas (1973), this is a 'scientisation' of politics, while for Bell (1973) it is a sign of 'technocracy'. Relatedly, the growth of medical expertise has been seen as resulting in a 'medicalisation' of social life, an incorporation of ever more areas of life under the medical gaze as objects of technical medical intervention (Brint 1994). The apparent neutrality of expertise obscures its character as power and can help to legitimate contentious policies and decisions. Expert knowledge works this way because of the knowledge-gap between experts and those who depend on them.

The expansion of state activity in the post-war period drew more and more areas of expertise into state policy and administration. Teachers, social workers, nurses, medical technicians, and a whole range of statisticians, economists, and other academics grew in number under the aegis of state planning and collective provision, and they did so while pursuing strategies of 'professionalism' that modelled their occupational autonomy on that of the established professions. Opposition came from these established professions, which saw threats to their own power, and the concern of state authorities to subordinate expertise to their own priorities and interests. In many areas, then, expertise became structured into hierarchical divisions of labour and many occupations had to organise their expertise in semi-professional ways.

From the 1970s many societies faced a growing fiscal problem of maintaining high levels of state expenditure and a growing disenchantment with the project of social planning for collective provision that was increasingly seen as having produced inefficiencies and failures. This lay behind the development of New Right liberalism from the 1970s and led governments to confront even the established professions and to attempt to limit their autonomy. In the name of 'deregulation' there was, in fact, a 're-regulation' of the professions, a restructuring of the relationship between state agencies and expert monopolies. Such policies

> have modified or promise to change long-standing work practices, in law, medicine and higher education. They have transformed relationships between solicitors and barristers, solicitors and estate agents, bankers and estate agents, accountants and solicitors, etc. As the effects of such policies work through the system they also reconstitute networks of expert/official discourse, creating new institutional forms such as medical audit and academic appraisal. A further effect of the policies has been to shift the established boundaries between 'neutral' expertise and politics, so repoliticizing issues once safely consigned to the expert's domain. (Johnson 1993: 146)

6
Protest and Collective Mobilisation

The relative merits of elitist and pluralist views of power have mainly been explored through considerations of the formally organised interest groups, pressure groups, and political parties that comprise stable and established political systems. These voluntary associations – 'parties' in Weber's sense of that word – are seen as representing and articulating interests in their attempts to influence the political decisions that are taken by state agencies. Pluralist theorists have emphasised that parties in government face the countervailing actions of 'veto groups', and they have often seen these resulting in balanced power relations and relatively orderly processes of policy formulation and change.

Even those who have highlighted processes of nondecision-making and the mobilisation of bias, have not generally considered the part played by counteracting groups that challenge established structures of power and attempt to bring about social and political reconstruction. Rebellions, revolutionary transformations, and collectively organised forms of violent action raise issues for power analysis quite distinct from those that have been considered in chapter 3. While 'parties' are groups that follow conventional, institutionalised patterns of political participation, protest groups are organised around collective resistance to the very structures that underpin party politics. Protest is most likely to occur whenever significant social interests are not incorporated into a stable structure of pressure politics. Indeed, a state that succeeds in institutionalising pressure politics but minimises mass participation may help to produce an accumulation of discontent that feeds oppositional acts of resistance (Gamson 1975: 6). Protest is most likely to be successful in its goals when the state at which it is aimed is weak. When a state's legitimacy or its ability to wield its coercive powers is weak, relative to the forces counteracting against it, the chances of protest action being successfully mobilised and exercised are much higher than in other circumstances (Skocpol 1979).

Protest is counteraction that is organised into cohesive and solidaristic forms of collective action. This has often been seen in terms of the formation and development of social movements. Marxists, for example, have seen the working class as engaging in forms of collective resistance to state power that develop its revolutionary consciousness and produce a progressively radicalised labour movement. More recent theories, however, have attempted to explore the emergence of new social movements of protest concerned with gender and sexuality, race and ethnicity, and the natural environment. They have looked at the interests, identities, and institutions that shape the social groups involved in these areas and turn some of them from a politics of pressure to a politics of protest.

Structures of Collective Action

Collective action takes a variety of forms, not all of which are relevant to collective protest. The most general term that can be used to describe a form of collective action, from the most to the least formal, is 'group'. Formal groups are typically referred to as 'organisations', and when dealing with contemporary power groups it is useful to distinguish between 'associations' and other types of organisation. Associations are rationally structured organisations that are instrumentally oriented towards the attainment or promotion of specific goals or purposes. Examples of associations are political parties, trades unions, and other formal organisations concerned with the promotion of particular interests or values. These associations differ from the less formal groups that may also be involved in political action – clubs, reading groups, social circles, friendship cliques, families, and work groups – as well as more abstract and anonymous collectivities such as mobs, crowds, and audiences.

Of all the various kinds of association, those most relevant to protest action are voluntary or membership associations rather than commercial, employing organisations. Voluntary associations claim to represent or to speak on behalf of particular constituencies, whether they be the potential supporters of their programmes or those who will benefit from their actions. Their criteria of membership relate to their goals, and their recruitment practices help to determine their size relative to the overall size of their constituency: this ratio is often referred to as their 'density of membership'.

Associations are not the same as social movements. A 'movement', according to the *Oxford English Dictionary*, is a body of persons with a common object, but this meaning is specified as referring to a body that is something other than simply an association. It is larger, more extensive, and more diverse; and it is termed a 'movement' in order to emphasise its involvement in action, in motion. A movement cannot be seen simply in terms of its members' occupancy of established and relatively static positions in a given structure. It is an extended social grouping that acts beyond the conventional routines of politics. While an activist association might plausibly be termed a movement on this strict definition, it seems more useful to restrict the term to broader groupings that result from the coalescence, federation, and alliance of activist associations with other groups.

The term 'social movement', then, can be seen as referring to networks of associations, groups, and individuals that are allied with each other through sharing a particular programme of action or sense of identity. In the words of Diani, social movements are 'networks of informal interactions between a plurality of individuals, groups, and/or organisations, engaged in a political or cultural conflict, on the basis of a shared collective identity' (1992: 13). Social movements have less clearly defined and generally more diverse goals than do associations, and they tend to follow more fluid and fragmentary programmes of action.

A women's movement, for example, might include a number of separate pressure and campaign associations, informal reading and consciousness raising groups, political parties, and individuals. Similarly, labour movements have included political parties of the left, trades unions, cooperatives, clubs, street-corner meetings, and other organisations and institutions of established working-class communities. Such movements are, then, loose but solidaristic networks of individuals, groups and organisations that are united by shared interests, a sense of collective identity, and perhaps a common ideology.

It is important, then, to distinguish between a social movement and the various associations that may be parts of it. While an association has a structure of internal leadership and can be more or less bureaucratic in its organisation, this is not typically the case with a social movement. An association is a centralised, and often hierarchical, form of collective action. A social movement has a more decentralised, flatter form. A particular association may predominate in a social movement – as socialist and labour parties have often done in labour movements – but the leadership of such a party does not constitute the formal leadership of the larger movement. Indeed, it can be quite misleading to talk about the leadership of a movement when many are quite decentralised or even fragmented. Environmental movements, for example, have become recognised and important elements in contemporary politics, and many are engaged in transnational actions, but it is doubtful if it is possible to speak of them as having 'leaders' at either a national or a global level.

Social movements may, of course, develop the kinds of leadership structures that make them into true associations in their own right – at which point, of course, they should no longer be seen as social movements in the sense that I have defined that term. Similarly, an established association may fragment into a myriad of allied groups and so be more usefully treated as a social movement. These possibilities of transformation between association and movement have led some commentators to see social movements simply as recently formed alliances that have not had a chance to settle down into formal, associational politics. Thus, Wrong holds that social movements are 'newly mobilized or mobilizing collectivities that have recently acquired a heightened sense of solidarity focused on a political demand without yet having produced a specialized permanent leadership and organization claiming to represent a larger following through routine channels and institutionalized procedures' (Wrong 1979: 154). While the temporal dimension in this definition may be somewhat misleading, this emphasis on the possible development of a movement into an association is very important.

Some associations seek only limited changes and may become involved in the politics of pressure. Others, however, are oriented in more activist ways towards fundamental changes in social structures or in resource distributions. These are 'challenger' or 'protest' associations. Tilly (1978), for example, holds that the politics of pressure occurs where contenders for positions of command and for involvement in decision-making seek simply to enter the established political system and to remain within it. Pressure associations may exchange resources with each other and build coalitions and alliances, but they do so in order to achieve power through their incorporation into policy networks of the kind that I looked at in chapter 3. This pressure tends to be 'competitive': it is based on claims to resources that are controlled by others, who are regarded as rivals in the same political contest. Pressure is the action of those who have 'achieved recognition of their collective rights to wield power over the government, and have developed routine ways of exercising those rights. They are members of the polity' (Tilly 1978: 125). Protest action, on the other hand, is the noninstitutionalised contention of collective actors. Protest groups are not legitimate and accepted 'members' of the political system: they are 'challengers' that 'contend without routine or recognition' (1978: 125). In a similar vein, Tarrow sees protest as contentious collective action, action that is 'used by people who lack regular access to institutions, act in the name of new or unaccepted claims and behave in ways that fundamentally challenge this' (1994: 2).

Melucci has defined any form of collective action that involves solidaristic conflict and that poses a challenge to the system in which it takes place as a 'social movement' (Melucci 1996: 28), but such a definition loses sight of the important distinction between an association and a movement.[1]

Some collective protest actions are 'reactive', while others are 'proactive'. Reactive protest involves the reassertion of established claims that are seen to have been threatened or violated by those in command or by some rival group. Reactive protest groups aim to re-establish what they have lost or to protect themselves from future loss. Proactive protest action, on the other hand, asserts claims that have not previously been exercised, aiming to open up new areas of contention over advantages and disadvantages (Tilly 1978: 144–7).

Social movements mobilise power for a variety of purposes, and a protest movement is a social movement whose programme and constituent associations pose a challenge to the established social order. The 'challenge' that is involved in a protest action involves the solidaristic organisation of people in pursuit of shared interests that conflict with those of others and whose satisfaction requires a restructuring of the system in which they are acting. Their action breaches the 'limits of compatibility' of the system and points beyond 'the range of variability in systemic states that enables a system to maintain its structure' (Melucci 1996: 24).

Della Porta and Diani (1990: 168–70) have argued that, because of the challenge that is posed to established structures of power, protest actions must use unconventional methods to influence a decision-making process and will generally operate through indirect channels of influence. Their methods tend to be novel or dramatic in some way and are, at the very least, outside the established norms and so are likely to be seen by non-participants as deviant acts. Protest groups rely on the use of petitions, boycotts, demonstrations, strikes, occupations, sit-ins, and other unconventional methods of counteraction. If particular protests come to be recognised and accepted, some of these methods may eventually become accepted elements in a repertoire of legitimate political action. Most, however, remain beyond the bounds of acceptability. Many of these unconventional means rest upon a complete abandonment of any commitment to more conventional means, and their use may lead protestors to contemplate engaging in violent or forceful acts. The exclusion of associations and movements from direct channels of decision-making also means that protest groups are likely to seek to work at a more general level by changing the climate of public opinion, perhaps through the use of the media of mass communications.

Theories of Organised Protest

Protest groups engage in counteraction on the basis of their size and their solidarity, their density of membership being a critical indicator of these aspects of group structure. They mobilise their members in a counteraction that is aimed at transforming established structures of power and that is more likely to be successful when the group is large and solidaristic. The classic theoretical discussions of protest are Marxist theories of revolution and the functionalist and interactionist theories of 'collective behaviour'. These have sought to relate collective mobilisation to the structural conditions that generate capacities for action and the forms of consciousness through which that action is organised. Where Marxists have stressed the rational character of protest, theories of collective behaviour have stressed its irrationality.

In Marxism, proletarian revolution is seen as the collective action of a working class, and as expressing the shared interests that result from its structural location in class relations. Structured fields of relations and the distributions of resources that they generate set the conditions under which people act, and it is class relations that Marxists see as the most important constraints on action. Patterns of class constraint, then, define the interests around which the members of the various classes will mobilise. For classical Marxism, it is the exploitative relationship of antagonistic interests between capitalists and proletarians that drives the proletariat into counteraction against the capitalist bourgeoisie. Through their counteraction, their class consciousness is radicalised and their protest becomes ever more revolutionary in character. Workers are brought together in ever larger numbers in large factories and places of employment, and their shared experiences at work and in the single-class communities in which they live produce a solidarity and consciousness of shared interests that underpins rational political protest at the structure of class relations. The associations and groups that form a labour movement, then, are driven towards revolutionary protest as an inevitable long-term consequence of the development of class relations.

Theories of so-called 'collective behaviour' (Smelser 1963) developed in parallel with the pluralist theory of pressure. Where pluralism was concerned with the 'normal', institutionalised processes of rational political action, collective behaviour theories focused on the 'deviant' forms of political action that occur outside the established institutions. Such collective behaviour was seen as 'irrational', as an emotionally organised response to strains generated by processes of social disorganisation and social dislocation. Institutionalised pressure, in the era of the 'end of ideology', is instrumental and strategic, but non-institutionalised protest is shaped by non-rational belief systems and by emotional commitments.[2] This view denied the rationality of mass and radical protest actions, which were seen simply as the emotional mobilisation of mobs and crowds in panics, manias, and crazes.

Both of these theories of collective mobilisation recognised that there were particular structural conditions involved in the generation of collective action, but they gave inadequate accounts of the specific ways in which this action was shaped. Marxism, which has concerned itself only with labour movements and class action, has employed a deterministic model of the links between structure, consciousness, and action, and has largely ignored the factors of social integration that mediate between structural contradictions and consciously organised actions. Collective behaviour theory, on the other hand, has simply seen protest action as the irrational and emotional expression of social breakdown. It, too, has ignored the specific links between structure and action. The strengths of both theories lie in their attempts to highlight the conditions that underpin the advantages and disadvantages enjoyed by different groups and that generate the interests that mobilise them to change these conditions. In both cases, however, there is a very weak understanding of the conditions under which mobilisation can occur, and neither can be seen as providing an adequate account of the forms of counteraction involved in protest.

More recent theories, however, have moved beyond this impasse by giving far more emphasis to the rational dimensions of collective action and to the ways in which this action is culturally and institutionally organised. The three main theoretical perspectives that have influenced recent debates are those stressing interests and the mobilisation of resources, cultural meanings and the construction of identities, and social institutions and the structure of political opportunities. The first two of these approaches are particularly concerned with the forms in which issues are expressed, and they stress, respectively, the needs that groups have to mobilise their resources for action and to construct the identities that can sustain this. The third theoretical approach is concerned rather more with the structural conditions that allow issues to emerge and the opportunities that are provided for their expression.

A stress on the part played by interests and resources has most often been seen as characteristic of a 'resource mobilisation theory'. Advocates of this theory focus on the strategic rationality of collective actors and on their ability to mobilise their members in the instrumental pursuit of benefits and outcomes that will advantage them in some way. Actors are seen as requiring or desiring certain resources and, therefore, as being dependent upon those who control these resources or opportunities to acquire them (McCarthy and Zald 1977; see also Oberschall 1973). Resources are subject to processes of bargaining, competition, and conflict among actors. Through these processes they can be accumulated and distributed, so enhancing or diminishing the powers of the groups that hold them. Collective action involves the pooling and mobilising of resources in relation to the pursuit of a collective goal. It is through control over resources that collective actors can employ forms of corrective influence in relation to others, and often over their own members.

Some advocates of resource mobilisation theory adopt a strict rational-choice model of action and have, therefore, to resolve the so-called 'free-rider' problem (Olson 1965; see also the discussion in Scott 2000a). This is the problem of how groups can attract and maintain the support of those who can gain benefits or advantages through the actions of the association, despite the fact that they are not active members. The poor, for example, benefit from a redistribution of income and welfare benefits, even if they are not members of protest associations that force such policies on a government. The problem faced by a rational-choice theory is that if everyone took a rational view of whether or not to join an association or movement, then no-one would find it profitable to participate in collective action. If this is the case, then why does collective action ever occur? A free rider – one who does not join – can gain only because others are motivated, in part, by an apparently non-rational obligation to act in pursuit of a collective interest. Thus, resource mobilisation theorists must rely on other theoretical approaches if they are to explain the building of the solidarity and commitment that makes collective mobilisation a viable strategy of protest (Elster 1989).

An association's capacity to mobilise depends on the social closure that exists around those who form its constituency and the degree of solidarity and cohesion that it can build within those boundaries. Where rational considerations and corrective influence may be insufficient, persuasive power may be more effective. Persuasive influence allows the leaders of an association to trade on a sense of obligation and commitment among the mass membership. Arendt (1959) held that the diversity and conflict that characterise any social group can be overcome through persuasive speech that can build a sense of community and allow people to act in concert. Solidarity, then, is formed through what Habermas (1981a and b) calls 'communicative action': through the building of shared understandings, people are able to establish a consensus over the actions that they will jointly undertake. It is through communication that collective decisions can be produced and legitimated.

As the possibilities for both persuasive influence and corrective influence in an association are generally rather limited, they are most likely to be effective when they operate together. Groups that can establish specific benefits for their members and, more particularly, for their active adherents, for example, are better able to persuade them to become or to remain involved in collective action. An association that has, through processes of signification and legitimation, established clear boundaries and a sense of identity among its members, and that strengthens this through building dense and cohesive networks of relations among them, has a high degree of closure and a strong capacity for collective action (Tilly 1978).

This resolution of a central problem in resource mobilisation theory – the problem of the free rider – points to its close articulation with the second theoretical approach identified. This approach, stressing cultural meanings and the construction of identities, draws on the general framework of symbolic interactionism. Advocates of this approach hold that the successful establishment of collective forms of action, and the practical success of these actions, depends upon the construction of shared identities from which the members of associations can derive a feeling of solidarity and can be persuaded to participate in joint actions (Gusfield 1963; Eyerman and Jamison 1991; Melucci 1996). Culture provides the symbolic resources on which people draw to interpret their worlds and build strategies of action. Problems are not simply given and do not impel people, inexorably and inevitably, towards collective action in pursuit of their solution. Experiences are shaped by the cultural contexts in which they occur, and the subjectively recognised interests that motivate them are the products of processes of cultural construction.

Collective action, then, is more likely when individuals identify values and ideals that they feel they have in common with each other and that differentiate them from those who are the targets of their protest. Consciousness of kind and consciousness of difference are mobilised into distinct organisational self-identities that motivate the members of associations and movements to act in support of their aims and to join in their efforts to persuade others of their importance. The self-identity of an association, for example, may specify connections with other groups and with unattached individuals in a wider constituency who share the feelings that underlie the organisational identity and who encourage and support the actions of the association, so embedding it in a wider social movement.

Shared memories and experiences, rituals, and recurrent activities are the bases on which the identity and individuality of a group can be constructed. Shared and collectively organised narratives generate particular images and definitions that can be used in constructing the everyday meanings – the public and hidden transcripts (James Scott 1990) – that inform people's actions. Of particular importance are narratives of historical continuity that link the current form of an association or movement to those whom it regards as its predecessors and whose traditions or programme it aims to continue. The groups that formed the women's movements of the 1960s and 1970s, for example, saw themselves as the inheritors and developers of the ideals of earlier 'first-wave' feminism.

Through the construction of collective identities, then, groups can build and reinforce the connections and contacts that allow the communication of values, ideals, and information and that serve as a basis for building trust and solidarity among their members and supporters. It is on this basis that their leaders can engage in a persuasive effort to mobilise people to engage in moral crusades and other forms of symbolic protest. Protest, I have argued, is that form of collective action that involves common interests or goals whose pursuit challenges an existing social order. Central to the mobilisation of protest is the establishment of the solidarity and sense of shared identity that allows the building of the consciousness and closure that can sustain collective action over a period of time.

The third approach to collective mobilisation that I have identified operates at a slightly different level. It is concerned with the social institutions and structured opportunities within which collective mobilisation takes place, and it is sometimes referred to as the 'political process approach'. Its focus is on the environment within which particular groups operate; on the political framework of social relations and social institutions through which their protests take place (Tarrow 1994). Neither the rational pursuit of interests nor the construction of collective identities take place in a social vacuum. They are shaped by the institutional and relational structures that set the conditions under which they occur. The bias inherent in these structures (Schattschneider 1960) restricts or enhances the opportunities that associations and movements have to pursue their goals and to secure particular outcomes.

New interests and issues must always be expressed through inherited structures and modes of thought, even where they challenge these and seek to change them. Those involved in protest actions, Tilly argues, draw on the available 'repertoire of contention' (Tilly 1978; 1986), the public conventions of action that tell them what, from among the social stock of familiar forms of action, is most likely to be effective. Similarly, their chances of success vary with the ways in which their actions are filtered through the established possibilities for communication, organisation, and discussion. Repertoires of contention are the collective sediments of processes of learning and emulation. Protest movements that seek to maximise their chances of success will try to innovate in an attempt to secure a tactical advantage. Successful innovations are emulated by others and so become part of the regular routines of collective action, and it is in this way that an available stock of routines is developed and transformed over time. Associations and movements draw on the existing repertoire and, through their successful innovations, they contribute to its transformation.

The Development of Protest

Tilly and Tarrow have set out a powerful historical framework for understanding the development of collective action. The crucial period in the development of protest associations and movements in Europe and the United States, they argue, was the late eighteenth century, when the transition from local to national organisation first became a marked feature of protest actions. From then until the middle of the twentieth century, the politics of protest was overwhelmingly national in scope, and protest groups focused their actions on challenges to nation states. In the early modern period, however, protest was localised and particularistic, operating through retributive actions and, on occasion, riot: typical repertoires of action included noisy expressions of disapproval ('charivari' and 'rough music'), field invasions, food riots, and seizures of grain. From the late eighteenth century, however, national associations and movements had emerged and adopted new repertoires, including rallies, marches, demonstrations, public meetings, and strikes. In contrast to the localised repertoires of contention, these new repertoires are 'modular' (Tarrow 1994: 33): they are transferable – more or less intact – from one context of action to another and so can spread more effectively. The key events in the consolidation of these new routines of action were the reform struggles and revolutions that swept Britain in the 1830s and other parts of Europe from 1848.

The underlying conditions that made such national protest action possible include, most importantly, the technology of communication and the encouragement of new forms of association (Tarrow 1994: 58). Commercial print technology moved communication beyond the face-to-face relations of local villages and neighbourhoods and allowed the formation of an autonomous public opinion through books, newspapers, and pamphlets. This use of technology was most strongly encouraged by the new and more 'public' associations that became possible with the growth of clubs, coffee houses, and committees (Habermas 1962). The development of nation states – as I showed in chapter 2 – provided opportunities for national social movements that sought to change state policies. Such demands for change occurred at the same time that states were spending their resources on the creation of a framework of citizenship through building standing armies, roads, welfare agencies, and educational institutions. States therefore became targets of action and arenas of contention, with industrial workers becoming the leading elements in protest. These movements and associations are, it can be said, 'antisystemic' (Arrighi et al. 1989: 30).

Two landmark studies show the development of these forms of collective protest: Tilly's study of France during the period 1830–1960 (in Tilly et al. 1975)[3] and Gamson's (1975) study of 'challenging groups' in the United States over the period 1800–1945. Tilly's study used a wide range of documentary sources to explore the parameters of protest, while Gamson looked in more detail at a sample of case studies. Gamson drew his sample, of 53 groups, from the 500–600 challenging groups that he was able to identify, ranging from those with relatively modest reformist views to those with more radical and sometimes revolutionary aims. The sample included such associations as the International Workingmen's Association (the First International), the American Anti-Slavery Society, the Christian Front Against Communism, and the German–American Bund. Protest associations of the period that did not figure in the sample included such well-known organisations as the International Workers of the World (the Wobblies) and the Ku Klux Klan.

Tilly looked initially at the structural conditions that allow the emergence of collective protest. These conditions were those generated by the processes of industrialisation and urbanisation that contemporary societies were undergoing:

> An urban-industrial class structure gradually emerged from a class structure based on land and locality. The new structure relied on control of capital or labour rather than on landed wealth. It separated owners and managers of large formal organizations (factories, governments, schools) from their employees. It emphasised positions in the national labour market over local attachments, and gave exceptional rewards to technical expertise. Periods of urban-industrial growth accelerated this transformation of the class structure. (Tilly et al. 1975: 45)

Tilly was concerned to document the levels of violence and radicalism that resulted from these structural changes. There was, he argued, no once and for all increase, but neither was there a progressive rise. Instead, there were fluctuations with periodically high levels. Major peaks of violence occurred in 1848, 1900, 1930, and 1950, and Tilly sees these as effects of short-term structural changes. As industry and urbanism spread, the advantages and resources associated with them were directed away from groups that, nevertheless, retained a degree of internal organisation and a capacity for collective mobilisation. Long-term continuation of their protests, however, was undermined by the similarly short-term effects of urbanism and industry on their capacities for action – increased geographical and occupational mobility, community breakdown, and so on made it more difficult to sustain the solidarity and cohesion needed for effective collective protest (in Tilly et al. 1975: 83–4).

There was, then, no long-term increase in either the amount of violence or the level of collective protest. What changed with industrialisation and urbanisation were the *forms* of collective action. The strikes, demonstrations, and other actions that made up the repertoire of contention became shorter in duration and larger in scale between the nineteenth and twentieth centuries. They did not last for so long as their predecessor forms of action, but they involved many more people. The typical protest event of the 1830s involved families in the same locality joining reactively in one day of action after another. The typical event of the 1930s, however, involved formal associations engaged in single-day shows of strength, often organised by a political party that was able to mobilise the felt solidarities of national movements of workers.

Gamson's main concern in his study was with the successes and failures that marked such events and the actions of the groups involved in them. Associations show varying degrees of success in achieving their goals, and many are outright failures. Gamson sees investigation into the conditions responsible for success and failure as the most useful way of assessing their power in collective mobilisation. 'Success' is marked by the recognition and 'acceptance' of an association as a valid spokesperson for a constituency and, in consequence, an enhanced ability to secure its advantages. This may involve, for example, securing new legislation or a structural change in government. Associations that continue to operate may either continue their radical oppositional struggles or attenuate their goals and become incorporated into an established system of pressure. Associations may cease to operate for a number of reasons: they may successfully achieve their goals and so disband or merge with another group, or they may fail in their goals and so be unable to sustain their protest. The particular outcome depends on the ease or difficulty with which different constituencies can be mobilised, as well as on the responses of established political authorities and the political structures in which the associations operate. Concessions and recognition by state authorities and by existing pressure groups, for example, may allow a feared protest association to be co-opted or incorporated, and this may lead to a dilution of its demands.

The recognition and acceptance of a protest association, Gamson argues, occurs when the established authorities consult it and involve it in negotiations, and when it is regularly involved in a particular policy domain and its pressure networks. There is, that is to say, a recognition of the *legitimacy* of involving the organisation on a regular basis in the policy process. Rejection by the established authorities and the denial of any legitimate part in the exercise of power, on the other hand, tends to encourage a protest organisation to persist in its opposition and, perhaps, to raise its demands. The *de facto* inclusion of an association, on the other hand, occurs where radical or revolutionary groups are rejected by established authorities but are able to secure a place for themselves in the political or opinion-forming process through their electoral success or through sheer force. Such a protest association may be able to secure some of its goals, despite the overt opposition of the established authorities.

Gamson found that over a half of the protest associations successfully generated the desired advantages or outcomes for their constituents, and almost the same number achieved either full recognition or *de facto* inclusion. Overall, two in five of the associations that he studied had achieved both some kind of recognition or inclusion *and* advantages for their members (1975: 34, 37). A slightly smaller number of associations experienced complete collapse, achieving neither political success nor their desired outcomes.

The chances of success, Gamson found, were closely related to the nature of the goals of the association. He notes that the greater and more radical is the challenge posed by an organisation, the less likely it is to succeed (see also Ash 1972). Associations with revolutionary and wide-ranging goals succeed fully only if these can be translated into narrower, discrete goals that can be achieved piecemeal. An association that fails to act in this way can achieve some success only if it eschews the search for recognition and uses tightly organised collective power to pursue a strategy aimed at displacing the existing members of an elite (Gamson 1975: 41). Such mobilisation is difficult to sustain over any time, and it is also difficult to focus. About one third of the associations studied by Gamson sought a change in the composition of the established political leadership, but only two of these were at all successful and none had any real success in gaining new advantages for their constituencies.

Despite this general relationship between success and the moderation of goals, radical and revolutionary groups have often been able to achieve success in their quest for structural change. A revolution occurs as a result of a long process in which groups become disenchanted with a political leadership or government regime and enter into serious contention with it, aiming at its overthrow through violent or coercive action and the implementation of a programme of social change (Calvert 1992: 17). Central to a revolutionary movement, therefore, is an association that is small enough and cohesive enough to guide the actions of other groups towards the aims set out in its programme. A revolutionary movement is likely to be successful only if the leadership of such an association can take advantage of the opportunities provided for it by social conditions and the actions of the established leadership.[4]

While there were no revolutionary transformations of American society in the period studied by Gamson, such changes have occurred outside the United States. Some writers have suggested that revolutions are especially likely to occur in crisis periods when international hegemony breaks down and controls over peripheral and semi-peripheral nations, and control over members within core states, are seriously weakened (Halliday 1999: 178; see also Skocpol 1979). When international instability is followed by a period of warfare, post-war revolutions are especially likely to occur and to have significant chances of success. Thus, the First World War was followed by revolutions and radical protests in Russia and Germany, the Second World War was followed by the Chinese and Vietnamese revolutions, and the decline of US hegemony from the mid-1970s was associated with a spate of Third World revolutions. There were fourteen such revolutions in the period 1974–80 – including those in Angola, Nicaragua, and Iran – compared with none at all in the period 1962–74 (Halliday 1983). Similarly, the sudden collapse of the Soviet Union and its hegemony across East and Central Europe in 1989 led eventually to the overthrow of all the pro-Soviet regimes of Europe.

One of the key considerations in the study of protest associations has been the effect of a group's size on its mobilised power. It is, of course, difficult to measure the size of a group and to decide on what is to count as 'big' or 'small', as this depends on the particular context in which an association is operating. Nevertheless, certain conclusions have been drawn. The US associations studied by Gamson ranged in size from fewer than 1,000 to many millions of members – the median size was 10,000. Larger than average associations were more likely to achieve recognition or inclusion, but they were barely any more successful in achieving advantages for their members.

This points to the importance of the argument of Michels (1911), who found that the leaders of some large associations developed a stake in maintaining their associations and their own positions within them. Drawing on ideas from elitist theory, Michels showed how a gulf can develop between those in positions of leadership and the rank and file membership of an association. Michels' 'iron law of oligarchy' held that elected officials in socialist parties and similar radical groups tend to develop interests and career concerns distinct from those of the mass membership, and seek to maintain their privileges and advantages within the organisation by insulating themselves from their constituents. As officials with powers of command and an interest in maintaining their power, they find that they have a great deal in common with the state officials to whom they present the demands of their organisation. Their interests as an established leadership group encourage them to seek acceptance from other established groups rather than to continue to pursue the more radical goals that they were initially elected to pursue. The radicalism of the association or movement is weakened by this accommodation of their leadership with the powers that be. Leaders of socialist parties and trades unions, then, tend to become committed to the politics of pressure, and they may even become part of the circulation of personnel around the interlocking positions of command. They become relatively conservative members of an established power elite rather than the leaders of a radical protest group, leaving the mass membership of their group in a disorganised or apathetic state or, perhaps, causing the rank and file to direct their discontent against their own leadership. The associations that are most likely to secure recognition by established elites are those that do so at the expense of the interests and goals of their members.

More important than size *per se* is the degree of solidarity that an association is able to achieve. This solidarity can be built through the exercise of power *within* the association, that is through the corrective and persuasive forms of influence highlighted in resource mobilisation and collective identity theories. Associations that are oriented towards a value or an ideal, rather than towards particular material benefits, are generally more likely to rely on persuasive influence, though revolutionary parties, for example, have often had recourse to force and manipulation to control their memberships. Gamson found a slight tendency for associations that relied on persuasive influence to mobilise their membership towards 'universalistic' goals to be less successful than those that used a greater variety of measures to mobilise their membership towards particular material benefits (Gamson 1975: 62–3).

Despite the importance of inducement and coercion, it did not appear that violence was always a guarantee of success. Just under one third of Gamson's challenger associations were involved in violent acts, either as the initiators of violence or in response to the violence of others. This violence ranged all the way from fights and beatings to lynchings and riots. Violent organisations were more likely to achieve recognition or inclusion than were non-violent ones, and they were also more likely to generate advantages for their members, especially if they were the initiators of the violence. The reasons for this success, Gamson argues, are not to be found in violence *per se*, but in the size of an association and the weakness of its opponents. Large associations are most likely to use violence against relatively weak opponents, as the chances of success are relatively high. Violence pays when the opponent is weak, but not when the opponent is strong and is able to mobilise counter-violence. For this reason, violence has rarely been used in the United States as a primary tactic by a protest association, and it is particularly rare when the protest is aimed directly at a branch of the state. Rather similar results were found for the use of other forms of force. As Gamson concluded, 'Virtue, of course, has its own intrinsic rewards. And a good thing it does too, since its instrumental value appears to be dubious' (1975: 87).

Globalisation and Protest

The second half of the twentieth century was a period of structural change that is comparable in scope and significance to the late eighteenth century, and many commentators have seen the old protest associations – predominantly those of industrial workers – as having been joined, or even replaced, by a variety of 'new' social movements (Arrighi et al. 1989). Transformations in work and employment such as the sectoral shift from production to services and consumption, the increased employment of women, the globalisation of business, and the extension of transnational capital flows and divisions of labour have destroyed many of the structural conditions that made possible the work-based solidarity of male industrial workers (Lash and Urry 1987; Castells 1996). At the same time, the break-up of long-established single-class communities has removed many of the non-work supports on which solidarity depended. As a result, labour movements and associations have faced increasing difficulties in mobilising workers for the collective exercise of counter-action against economic and political elites. Many such associations have found it easier to moderate their demands and to seek acceptance and recognition as part of an institutionalised structure of pressure.

These same changes have created fertile conditions for new associations and movements concerned with structural dislocations and their consequences: centralised states and interregional economic inequalities have strengthened nationalist and separatist movements; groups affected by inequalities in access to the public provision of housing and welfare have become major foci of protest; mass educational systems have generated conflict among students and those who are unable to enter labour markets; changes in both employment and in personal life have given a high profile to the issues of gender, sexuality, and citizenship that have been raised in the women's and gay movements; the perceived effects of new technologies have raised concerns that have been carried forward by environmental movements of various kinds; and changes in patterns of consumption and lifestyle have stimulated diverse associations and movements concerned with religious belief and personal identity.

Tarrow and Tilly saw the changes of the eighteenth century as resulting in the building of a new repertoire of contention, and it is possible to see current changes as leading to a similar transformation. Electronic communications through telephones, television, satellites, and the internet allow innovations in repertoire to spread more rapidly, and they provide new and more efficient bases for mobilisation and for the building of solidarity in protest groups. Most particularly, the growing globalisation of social life has stimulated a parallel globalisation of protest. These new patterns of power have been explored most clearly in discussions of the growth of environmental activism.

At the global level, networks of states and transnational agencies have become increasingly important, forming nascent policy communities and issue networks within globalised policy domains. As I showed in chapter 4, these transnational structures are far less stable and secure than their national counterparts, and there are correspondingly greater opportunities for radical protest groups to make their voices felt. According to Keck and Sikkink (1998), these global forms of political action can be regarded as forming 'transnational advocacy networks'. Their participants are, to be sure, subject to pressure, but routine pressure politics are not fully institutionalised at the global level. As a result, activists seek not only to influence policy outcomes, but also to transform the very terms of the policy debates. Protest groups 'are organised to promote causes, principled ideas, and norms, and they often involve individuals advocating policy changes that cannot be easily linked to a rationalist understanding of their "interests"' (1998: 8–9).

Global activists have been particularly likely among those groups that have been denied any effective political participation in the pressure politics of their home states (Kriesi et al. 1995). They have seen opportunities to mobilise transnational support aimed at making other states and agencies apply external pressure on their states. They have not emerged in all of the many policy domains found within the jurisdictions of nation states, but they have been especially extensive and important in such areas as human rights, the environment, women's rights, infant health, and the rights of indigenous peoples.

Widespread environmental concern has centred on such issues as the impact of transnational business enterprises on the global distribution of pollution, poverty, health, climate change, and other forms of technically-induced risk (Beck 1986). This has been expressed in protests over the uses of nuclear energy, the production of genetically-modified foods, animal protection and welfare, road building, and the depletion of natural resources. Since the early 1970s, a series of international conferences, summits, and commissions has linked these environmental issues to questions about strategies of economic development. Central to these debates has been the role of the IMF, the World Bank, and the World Trade Organisation (WTO), which have increasingly become the focus of protest by globally organised environmental organisations.[5]

The associations that form an increasingly globalised environmental movement include Greenpeace, Friends of the Earth, the Sierra Club, Earth First, numerous Green and Ecology parties, the World Wide Fund for Nature, and a whole variety of less formal organisations and groups. These are allied with each other through their overlapping membership, frequent communication, and joint campaigns. There is no single ideology, and various strands of environmental thought run through the movement, but its unity derives from a shared critical stance on the impact of economic enterprises and the role of political parties. They challenge the existing forms of environmental management by states and transnational agencies.

The possibilities of global protest are clear from such struggles as those against the World Bank in relation to the Three Gorges Dam in China, the Narmada Dam in India, and the Polonoreste rainforest scheme in Brazil (O'Brien et al. 2000). Initially, the World Bank attempted to operate through pressure politics and to create a policy community that would incorporate those who shared its views and whose institutional bias would marginalise other views and concerns. Many environmental groups drawn into this policy process, however, sought to maintain a distance from the Bank and directly mobilised public opinion by highlighting its failure to pursue sustainable development in its various projects. This shift in opinion forced the directors and managers of the Bank into a closer dialogue with members of the environmental associations, and it has slowly developed policies in relation to poverty, gender, and democratic participation, as well as the natural environment itself. Environmental groups have used their size and solidarity to make real gains in relation to their programmes.

Environmental groups have pursued a similar strategy in relation to the WTO, arguing that its promotion of free-trade policies has prevented any effective regulation of the effects of economic practices on the environment. The WTO, however, has not established any effective dialogue with environmental groups and it has not involved them in its framework of consultations. There has been no effective policy community. As a result, WTO institutions have been strongly challenged, becoming the objects of considerable contention. This challenge culminated in 'anti-capitalist' riots at the 1999 Ministerial Conference in Seattle and subsequent follow-on demonstrations in other economic centres where representatives of the WTO have met. These violent protests have been marked by a willingness to use direct action and sabotage in pursuit of environmental concerns, especially among 'deep ecology' groups. These patterns of protest show that the contemporary world system is increasingly characterised by a globalisation of anti-systemic protest movements (Arrighi et al. 1989), though the extent and the unity of these movements remains, as yet, very limited. They are transnational advocacy networks that challenge established national and trans-national agencies and that show little sign of any movement into institutionalised policy networks and the politics of pressure.

7
Interpersonal Power

My discussion of power has, so far, concentrated on issues of domination and of resistance to domination. I have looked at the structuring of power in and around authoritative associations such as states and business enterprises. The view of power set out in chapter 1, however, pointed also to the whole complex of power relations that occur within, between, and beyond formal structures of domination. Structures of domination are produced and reproduced through interpersonal, face-to-face encounters, and these interpersonal relations are bases of power that are analytically quite distinct from the formally institutionalised structures. Where structures of domination rest upon the organised positions or locations that people occupy in institutional and relational structures, patterns of interpersonal power derive from the personal characteristics and attributes that people have. These include their physical and psychological characteristics – which are, of course, shaped in part by the social positions that they occupy – and they also include the particular ways in which they can draw upon and enhance the resources attached to these social positions. Thus, an individual can derive power from their physical strength, their attractiveness to others, and their rhetorical abilities, but they may also derive power from their income and their political contacts. The recipient of income from a position of employment, for example, is able to use that income as a basis for power outside the formal contexts in which the income is generated.

Interpersonal power is not, however, without structure. While interpersonal power relations are diffused and often fluid, they can also be remarkably enduring and are embedded in larger structures such as those of class, ethnicity, and gender (Eichler 1981). The interpersonal power of a particular man, for example, reflects physical and personality characteristics that he has as a gendered individual of a particular ethnic and class background. His social habitus is the framework for his interpersonal power.

Feminist writers, for example, have recently highlighted the ways in which the differences, divisions, and inequalities that are associated with sex and gender are able to structure interpersonal relations in the private sphere as well as the formal and more impersonal structures of domination in the public sphere. They have pointed to the need to consider the body and bodily performance as central issues in power analysis, and they have drawn critically on Foucault's work on bodily power and power over bodies. Foucault's work on government and discipline stressed the need to look at the micropolitics of everyday life, at face-to-face interpersonal power relations that cannot be reduced to structures of command, constraint, and pressure.

While my general approach to power, with its emphasis on the elementary forms of corrective and persuasive influence, is applicable to interpersonal power as much as it is to domination, this does not mean that there are direct counterparts of command, pressure, constraint, and so on. The micropolitics of interpersonal relations require the use of additional concepts if the specific features of power and resistance in the proximal contexts of interpersonal relations are to be properly explored.

It is also important to look at the ways in which interpersonal power can be an essential element in patterns of domination. As I have argued, structures of domination are manifest in and through the interpersonal relations that reproduce and transform them. The powers of the president of a state, for example, are due to his or her personal characteristics, resources, and persuasive abilities as well as to the formal powers attached to the office. This is particularly clear in the form of power that Weber called 'charismatic authority'. This is a form of authority that results from particular individual, personal characteristics, but that has to be institutionalised in more formal structures of command if it is to persist over time. Fluid interpersonal relations based on charisma become institutionalised as structures of domination that then come to have a new relationship to the interpersonal relations of those involved in them.

In this chapter I will look at the elementary forms of interpersonal power, which lie in the bodily presence of human agents in their encounters and the particular resources that they can bring to them. I will concentrate on the theorisation of these processes by those interested in the gendering of power, though similar considerations apply to other forms of difference such as class, ethnicity, and age. I use this discussion as a way of exploring structures of patriarchal power, where public and private relations are brought together in interesting and complex ways. Household and family structures are the crucial contexts in which interpersonal power is honed and exercised, producing patterns of power that differ markedly from those that arise in the formal, public relations of the State and the economy that they, nevertheless, articulate with in determinate ways. Finally, I look at charismatic power and the dependence of formal, authoritarian powers of command on the dynamics of interpersonal encounters.

Power, Dependence, and Embodiment

As I showed in chapter 1, power relations can be seen as relations of principals and subalterns, each of whom pursues their own interests and advantages. The difference between a principal and a subaltern reflects the particular resources that the various participants are able to bring to their face-to-face encounters. The earliest and most important contributions to the study of interpersonal power came from the social–psychological work of those such as French and Raven (French 1956; French and Raven 1959; see also Lippitt 1952; Thibaut and Kelley 1959) who used specifically rational models of action, though their aim was to examine both corrective and persuasive forms of interpersonal causal influence.

These writers follow the view that power is the capacity to influence others, and so they see the overall power of an individual as the maximum possible influence that he or she can exert on others. A principal may choose, for whatever reason, to exert less than their full power, but they nevertheless retain the capacity in full (French and Raven 1959: 152). According to Emerson, this power is rooted in relations of dependence. One actor is dependent on another, he argues, whenever the attainment of his or her goals is facilitated by certain actions on the part of the other (Emerson 1962: 349). The other may, for example, control resources that will help the first person to do or to obtain what they seek (Secord and Backman 1964: 247). Typically, argues Emerson, a social relation will involve the mutual dependence of the participants, each actor being dependent – in greater or lesser part – on the other. Individuals seek to acquire the resources that they desire from those who control access to them, and the use of power in a social relationship therefore involves the implicit striking of a bargain or negotiation concerning these resources: there is an exchange of rewards and costs, threats, or promises aimed at coercing or inducing others to act in certain ways.

Social groups can be seen as composed of long and entwined chains of dyadic interdependence. Emerson sees the relative power of each actor as directly reflecting their overall dependence on each other in their relations. The power relations in these networks reflect the balance of dependence that is struck in each case. As each pair-wise link in the network involves inequality in this dependence and, therefore, a more or less unequal balance of power, a balance of power is rarely, if ever, an all-or-nothing matter. Each participant influences the other – resisting their power – to a greater or lesser extent. It is the social distribution of dependence that makes some actors principals and others subalterns. The power of a principal over a subaltern is, at its most general, equal to the dependence of the latter on the former (Emerson 1962: 350; see the critical elaboration of this in Hartsock 1983: Part I).

This kind of analysis points to the need to identify the possible 'bases' of power in interpersonal relationships. French and Raven (1959) identify three general bases of interpersonal power, two linked to resources and one to identification and commitment:[1]

- *Rewards.* The holding of rewards makes someone attractive to others because they have the ability to mediate access to things desired by them. They can grant 'positive valences' or they can remove or decrease 'negative valences'. Resources employed as rewards (actual or promised) lead the participants in a relationship to calculate the inducements and incentives involved in various alternative courses of action.
- *Punishments.* Resources can be used as punishments when they allow one person to mediate access to things that others seek to avoid. A punishing principal provides negative valences and removes or denies positive valences.
- *Identification.* Where one individual identifies with another, taking them as a reference group or point of reference for their own actions, they are likely to emulate them. The emulator becomes a subaltern by virtue of their identification with another whom they regard as a model, ideal, or simply as a persuasive example to follow. French and Raven see such subalterns as subject to 'referent power'.

As I argued in chapter 1, rewards and punishments are closely related as the two sides of the same phenomenon of calculation. They are the bases of what French and Raven call 'reward power' and 'coercive power', both involving the 'ability to manipulate the attainment of valences' (French and Raven 1959: 157). Attention must, therefore, be given to the distribution of those things that can serve as rewards and punishments in social interaction. Referent power, on the other hand, is not a calculative form of action but operates through persuasion and emulation. Referent power may, nevertheless, derive from reward power. Those who supply rewards – especially when they supply highly valued rewards – are likely to be seen as attractive and worthy individuals.

Over time, therefore, the provision of rewards builds up a commitment or loyalty that can be used as a basis for referent power. The exercise of coercion, on the other hand, tends to generate alienation and hostility, and this is an unlikely basis for identification. The key mechanism at work in these forms of interpersonal power is cognitive dissonance (Festinger 1957): one individual is likely to adjust his or her feelings towards those who grant or withhold the things that they value.

From this standpoint, then, the dependence of one actor on another in an interpersonal encounter varies with two factors: the importance that their goals have for them and the number and type of alternatives that are available to them. The first of these is the 'demand' variable. When a goal is of great importance to an actor, he or she will have a strong desire to obtain the necessary resources, and so will increase the demand for them. Conversely, a goal that is of little importance relative to other goals can be abandoned or marginalised, and the actor will reduce the overall demand for the resources. Other things being equal, demand is translated into dependence: the actor who strongly seeks resources controlled by another becomes, thereby, dependent upon that other. This dependence is modified, however, by the second, supply variable. Where there are few other ways in which the resources can be obtained, they are scarce. The dependence of actors on those who hold scarce resources, assuming these resources to be in demand, is high. On the other hand, where resources can easily be obtained elsewhere, it is difficult for stable relations of dependence to persist, and interpersonal power relations will be correspondingly weaker. The extent of a person's power, Emerson argued, is measured by the amount of resistance that has to be overcome in achieving what he or she wants. Other things being equal, a high level of dependence undermines the ability to resist. The formation of principals and subalterns in interaction, therefore, depends upon the interplay of supply and demand.

A married woman, for example, may depend on her husband for material support if she has no alternative sources of support available to her. She may, for example, have no capital of her own and few employment opportunities, depending on her husband's income for her own level and style of living. In these circumstances, the dependence of the woman is a basis for the man's power over her. The relative contribution of husbands and their wives to household decision-making, then, may depend on their relative contributions to household income (Blood and Wolfe 1960). Where a married woman is able to support herself in an acceptable way of life from her own resources, she has some capacity to resist the power of her husband. Wolfe (1959) suggested that a wife's power increases with employment outside the home and that, conversely, a woman with 'a strong need for love and affection' will have less power in her marriage because of her high dependence on her husband.

The balance of power and resistance may vary quite considerably with variations in dependence. One husband may completely dominate his wife in all spheres of her life, another may find it relatively easy to require her to clean the house but far more difficult to require unpaid secretarial services, while another may find his own life significantly circumscribed by his independently wealthy wife. The power of wives increases with the size of their income and the length of time that they have been in employment (Safilios Rothschild 1976). As Mulholland (1994) has shown, however, men often have other sources of power that enable them to capture control of their wife's resources and so reduce their capacity to resist.

Actors engage in a calculus of dependency to discover the balances of power that they face in the various situations that make up their lives, and Emerson held that a rational actor will try to alter any power relation that is to their disadvantage. Thus, subalterns will wish to reduce their dependence on principals. Imbalances in power–dependence relationships cannot always be altered, or can be altered only at great cost, and subalterns will remain relatively powerless. Emerson identified, however, four strategies that subalterns can sometimes employ to improve their situation:

- *Motivational withdrawal.* This involves a reduction in the subjective salience of a goal or interest, so devaluing the necessary resource that is controlled by a principal. This strategy reduces the demand.

- *Extending the range of supply.* In this strategy, a subaltern seeks to secure alternative sources of the necessary resource, so bypassing the person on whom they are currently dependent, this strategy increases the supply of the resource.
- *Coalition formation.* Here, the bargaining strength of the subaltern is enhanced by forming alliances with others in a similar situation. The allied subalterns can counterbalance the power of a principal.
- *Deference.* This involves establishing a new resource on which, it is hoped, the principal might become dependent and, therefore, less powerful. According status, prestige, or recognition to a principal, for example, may mean that he or she becomes dependent on the subaltern for continued recognition, partially reversing the overall power imbalance.

Further work by Emerson with Cook (Cook et al. 1983) has extended this argument from the case of dyadic, pair-wise relationships, such as that of husband and wife or parent and child, to larger groups such as whole families and school classes. These groups are modelled as 'exchange networks' using the techniques of social network analysis. In such models, the power available to people within their groups can be measured by their centrality within a pattern of interdependencies (Freidkin 1998). The connections among actors constitute an opportunity structure that constrains the possibilities of action that are open to the various group members. One key area of research has been the mapping of the various kinds of group structure that result (the chain, the star, and so on), which are seen as differing structures of power (Bavelas 1950).

Patriarchy, Sexuality, and Power

Interpersonal power is, in its most basic forms, proximal power. It is rooted in the bodily proximity of specific individuals and the possibilities that this offers for face-to-face encounters. It is not a matter of interchangeable individuals exercising powers attached to the social positions that they occupy, but of the personal attributes and characteristics of individuals – often derived from and shaped by their social positions – that are manifest in and through direct embodied encounters outside of those formal positions of authority. Bodily habitus – class habitus, racialised habitus, gender habitus, and so on – is central to interpersonal power, and its dynamics have been importantly developed in recent feminist writings and, in particular, by those who have been influenced by Foucault's (1976) account of the disciplining of bodies. These writings have sought to develop an understanding of power beyond the state and economy, especially in so far as it is integral to gendered social relationships.

The discussion of power was first seriously introduced to feminist thought by Kate Millet (1970) in her analysis of 'sexual politics'. Intimate relations of sexuality, love, and family, she argued, were, at the same time, relations of power that could be seen as the origin and foundation of gender divisions in many other areas of social life. It was in this sense that she saw 'personal' relations of intimacy in the private sphere as being central to the 'political' relations of public life. Cultural representations and values produce sexual differences of behaviour in family households and make them appear both obvious and natural, legitimating gendered forms of domination in other areas of social practice. However loving or sexually intimate these personal relations might be, they can also be seen as relations of exploitation and oppression through which control over money, property, domestic labour, and other household resources are organised (Barrett and McIntosh 1982). Many feminists have described these domestic power relations as relations of *patriarchy*. According to Delphy (1977), for example, patriarchal social relations are those that allow husbands to appropriate the unpaid domestic labour of their wives. She argues that the 'domestic mode of production' through which domestic labour is organised must be seen as a relational structure that has, as one of its conditions of existence, the social institutions of marriage and fatherhood that underpin patriarchy. It has been noted, however, that this point of view makes it difficult to distinguish patriarchy from sexist male domination. Both Sydie (1987) and Barrett (1980; see also Middleton 1974) have advocated the use of Weber's (1914) concept of 'patriarchalism' as a more all-encompassing idea, noting that patriarchalism denotes the power of a father over younger men as well as women within a family.[2] Patriarchalism is that particular form of traditional authority in which a father, as 'senior of the house' or 'sib elder', exercises full and complete personal power over all members of his household. The women living in the household (wives and daughters), together with their children, the unmarried sons of the patriarch, and domestic servants, are all subject to this power. It is personal power unencumbered by any formal rules and restrictions other than those of traditional custom and practice.

Patriarchalism in personal relations is the basis of patrimonial domination in the political and economic spheres. Power relations initially stretch beyond individual households as patriarchs grant land to their sons and other dependants for them to set up their own patriarchalist households under the overriding authority of the senior patriarch. In a fully developed system of patrimonialism, a patrimonial ruler operates across a territory with a subordinate staff of civil and military retainers and claims quasi-patriarchalist rights of authority over all who live within the territory. In such a system, the only effective challenge to the patrimonial leader can come from the nobility of military leaders that he builds up, and there is only a very restricted basis for any female participation in public activities (Sydie 1987: 72,75).

Barrett (1980: 250) noted, however, that patriarchalism and patrimonial authority are far from being typical features of the capitalist societies that have been the main focus of feminist discussions of patriarchy. There were elements of this strong patriarchalism in the Victorian view of the family and in Fascist ideology, but it has not been a normal or typical feature of contemporary societies. The sexism and gender divisions that exist in the private and the public spheres cannot be properly understood if they are simply equated with the patriarchalism of traditional systems. In some later reflections, however, Barrett (1988) modified her position somewhat and argued for a distinction between patriarchalism and patriarchy. The concept of patriarchy plays an important political and analytical function in highlighting the separate and distinct character of women's oppression: even in patriarchalism of the kind described by Weber, it is important to distinguish the oppression of women from the oppression of young men. 'Patriarchalism' is a specific form of traditional household relations, while 'patriarchy' is one structural element in this which may also be found in non-patriarchalist systems. Thus, contemporary forms of oppression by sex and gender may legitimately be described as relations of patriarchy, or perhaps 'neo-patriarchy' if their distinctiveness from traditional forms is to be emphasised (Mann 1986a). This position accords with that of Millet (1970), who saw patriarchy as a structure of relations that permeates many social contexts and not just the household. A patriarchal structure is one in which men as a category dominate women as a category; this domination is expressed in the generation of advantages for men and disadvantages for women (Murray 1995). The interpersonal power relations of patriarchy in the family are, then, integral to larger structures of patriarchy that shape the forms of domination that have been described in the previous chapters.

Patriarchalism is personal power that is ascribed to a father by virtue of his position in a male blood line, and this biological aspect of power has also been emphasised in many radical feminist discussions of contemporary forms of patriarchy (Millet 1970; Firestone 1971). They have seen women as shaped by their bodies and emotions, holding, for example, that women must recover or recapture their own bodies from their subordination to male power and must learn how to get in touch, autonomously, with their own biological characteristics. There has been an emphasis, for example, on the need for a more positive evaluation of the nurturing and caring activities that come 'naturally' to women.

Such views have often involved the idea that patriarchal power relations must be seen as biologically determined, and they have been much criticised for this explicit or implicit biological reductionism (see Barrett 1980: 12). The derivation of female attributes from an essentially female physique simply reinforces established ideas of male–female differences,

reversing the moral valuation of them that characterises patriarchal attitudes. In explaining social relations as mere reflexes
of biological conditions, such arguments ignore both the
specificity of the social and the extent to which biology is
socially constructed. The analysis of the mechanisms of interpersonal power and patriarchal relations has, therefore, been
most usefully advanced by those who have endeavoured
to build a sociology of gendered bodies through a critical
engagement with the ideas of Foucault. Foucault's work
suggested a way of conceptualising the body without transforming its material existence into a fixed biological essence.
These writers have explored the relationship between biological conditions and processes of social construction in the
generation of male power.

Gender differences are not seen simply as cultural imposi-
tions on pre-given biological sex differences, but as consequences of the social production of sex differences (Butler
1990). As McNay has argued, 'In relation to the body, power
does not simply repress its unruly forces, rather it incites,
instils and produces effects in the body' (1992: 38). Recognising the crucial part played by processes of social construction, Foucault emphasised the role of meanings and
ideas in defining embodied identities and forms of bodily
action. Sex and gender identities, for example, were seen as
shifting and unstable constructions, variably constrained by
the natural, fleshy characteristics of the body. Foucault's
analysis of the body begins from *sexuality* rather than from
sexual difference. Sex, he argued, is not a natural desire or
instinct, but is culturally constructed through relations of
power concerned with the regulation and control of bodies.
Feminists influenced by Foucault have shown that regimes of
power/knowledge organised by a discourse of femininity in
relation to other discourses of health and illness, deviance,
and pleasure have produced female bodies defined by their
reproductive capacities and by practices of mothering (Bland
1979). Similarly, male bodies have been constructed primarily in terms of sexual desires and urges and practices
of control. Thus, Hartsock (1983) has stressed the ways in
which this production involves a sexual-erotic form for gendered power relations. The cultural linkage between sex and

power structures eroticism around relations of opposition and domination, and this organisation of sexuality permeates all other gender relations.

The family lies at the heart of sex–gender differentiation and has to be seen as a mechanism of disciplinary power. Less formal and overtly coercive than the 'total' institutions studied by Foucault himself, it is, nevertheless, a system of productive power relations.[3] The patriarchal structures of the family household and the wider society do not, however, simply produce passive women as 'victims'.[4] McNay has suggested that Foucault moved closer to an understanding of the resistance of the active individual in the second and third volumes of his *History of Sexuality* (Foucault 1984a; 1984b), where he looks at the self rather than simply at the body. In this later part of his work, individuals were seen as actively constructing their own experience in dynamic relationships with those who exercise power over them. Women are active agents in these power relationships, and they can, and do, challenge them. Women and men are active participants – though not necessarily *equal* participants – in the construction of their gendered identities and their personal biographies: 'gendered identity is not simply stamped on individuals' bodies by inexorable external forces, but involves individual participation on a large scale' (McNay 1992: 72).

Such issues are highlighted in discussions of the control over money within households. Vogler and Pahl (1994) have usefully seen this in terms of various levels of control which they relate to general debates on power. In virtually all the systems of household management that they studied, one partner or another took overall responsibility for managing household income and spending. In 42 per cent of cases, women managed these resources, while in 25 per cent men were the financial managers (see also Pahl 1980; Morris and Ruane 1989). Such day-to-day management, however, did not necessarily coincide with the pattern of 'strategic control' within the household. Echoing studies of business management (Pahl and Winkler 1974), they saw strategic decisions as concerned with overarching structural issues: the domestic management system itself, the balance between personal spending and collective household expenses, and major items of expenditure. Day-to-day household management, then, was a delegated responsibility granted by the strategic controller.

Cultural discourses of masculinity and femininity, the patriarchal family, and the male breadwinner establish the basis for the dominant pattern of male strategic control in marital households (Vogler 1998: 697; see also Brannen and Moss 1991), though female and joint systems of strategic control also exist. Male strategic control tends to be associated with male management, while joint strategic control coexists with both male and female management systems. Female strategic control, on the other hand, occurred in only a very small minority of cases.

The system of strategic control determines the system of household management, Vogler argues, and they jointly establish a framework of taken-for-granted procedures that set an agenda for action – an institutionalised bias – and define certain issues out of the sphere of explicit decision-making. Women were especially disadvantaged in this. They were, for example, especially likely to experience deprivations, such as a lack of personal spending money, in female-managed systems where husbands controlled the level of their own spending and women had to cut corners to make ends meet (Vogler and Pahl 1994: 278–82). The chances that women had to counter male power depended crucially on their own income and employment and, therefore, on their degree of financial dependence on their husbands.

Interpersonal Power and Charismatic Authority

Formal, public relations of domination cannot be sharply separated from the informal relations of interpersonal power. Domination is always realised in and through interpersonal relations, and these can give a distinctive character to the pattern of domination. The nature of domination and the outcomes of its use will differ, for example, with differences in the class, gender, and ethnicity of those who occupy positions of power, and with the various personal characteristics that they bring to their social relations. Gendered and racialised patterns of command, as discussed in chapter 2, are examples of this interdependence of domination and interpersonal power, but it is also important to note that the precise ways in which power is exercised by its holder can also vary with the personality attributes of the power holder. What is particularly important to discuss here is the way in which such attributes can give rise to distinctive forms of authority. I will look, specifically, at how personality characteristics may result in structures of charismatic authority, and I will show how this enters into other forms of command.

Patriarchalist and bureaucratic structures of authority, Weber argued, are routinised, institutionalised aspects of social life. Charismatic authority, on the other hand, transcends day-to-day practical routines and is, by its very nature, *extraordinary*. Where patriarchalism and bureaucracy involve the holding of office, charisma operates through 'specific gifts of body and mind' that make an individual appear to be supernatural or out of the ordinary in some way. The word 'charisma' refers to something that is seen as a 'gift', a sign of favour, grace, or fortune, and its initial core meaning was a divine gift. Weber introduced the term 'charismatic domination' to refer to authority that occurs by virtue of such a gift. Weber finds this type of authority exemplified in such figures as religious prophets, shamans, oracles, pirate leaders, and warrior chiefs in relatively primitive societies.

Charisma is not, then, restricted to religious contexts, but is applicable wherever followers regard a leader as possessing a peculiar gift of personality that allows them to exercise extraordinary skills of leadership. The charismatic leader sees this gift as allowing the pursuit of a personal 'mission'. The leader 'seizes the task for which he is destined and demands that others obey and follow him [*sic*] by virtue of his mission' (Weber 1914: 1112). Thus, a charismatic leader exercises domination that is justified 'by virtue of a mission believed to be embodied in him' (1914: 1117). The charismatic leader is followed only in so far as this gift can be 'proved' through actions in pursuit of the mission, and the mission becomes impossible if the leader's personality cannot sustain the demonstration of the gift through appropriate and effective actions. The charismatic leader 'must work miracles, if he wants to be a prophet. He must perform heroic deeds, if he wants to be a warlord' (1914: 1114).

Weber focused attention, then, on the strong emotional bond that exists between charismatic leaders and their followers. The followers must have 'faith' in the charismatic leader, and when they have faith they will be devoted 'to the exceptional sanctity, heroism or exemplary character' (1920: 215) of the leader. They 'surrender' to an extraordinary quality of personality and personal magnetism in the leader, and they express this surrender in extreme personal loyalty, most typically in 'ecstatic' commitment and enthusiasm. It is important to note that it does not matter whether a person actually has some personality trait that sets them apart from others. What is crucial is that others *believe* him or her to have these characteristics. Charisma may, then, be a matter of impression management, of presenting an image that leads others to attribute some force of personality or personal magnetism. Thus, Bryman holds that charismatic leadership consists in 'relationships between leaders and followers in which, by virtue of both the extraordinary qualities that followers attribute to the leader and the latter's mission, the charismatic leader is regarded by his or her followers with a mixture of reverence, unflinching dedication and awe' (1992: 41). Such strong emotional commitments have to be renewed and reinforced through rituals that may involve singing and dancing, eroticism, the use of drugs, and other means of building up what Durkheim referred to as the 'collective effervescence' that sustains personal commitment.[5]

Charismatic leadership, in its pure form, is the polar opposite of permanent and formally organised domination. It does not use bureaucrats or officials, but those who have been 'called' to serve their leader in a personal capacity and who offer their unqualified attachment and loyalty. It can, therefore, operate without its administrators being motivated by the rational and systematic pursuit of income. The charismatic leader and his or her followers may be sustained, for example, by booty, charity, gifts, or voluntary donations.

Similarly, the power of a charismatic leader need not be expressed in formal commands and need not involve the use of material rewards and punishments. The expression of a wish or of a desire by a leader may simply be taken by the followers as if it were a command. The way that the leader lives – or is believed to live – for instance, may be taken as an example for all to follow. The smaller the group, the easier it is for it to operate in this way.

Although these pure forms of charismatic domination have no formal organisation, they are not simply amorphous patterns of interpersonal power. Charismatic authority has a social structure that is specifically adapted to its mission. There may, for example, be a 'charismatic aristocracy' of adherents or disciples who are chosen to serve as a loyal, personal staff for the leader. Weber emphasised, nevertheless, that there is a close connection between charisma and other forms of command. Pure charisma may become linked to specific social positions and so become fused with other forms of domination, operating as an integral element in a concrete historical pattern of authority. Indeed, Weber saw this as an inherent tendency for all pure forms of charisma, and as being especially likely when a charismatic organisation grows in size or has to secure successors to its current leadership.

What Weber meant was that purely personal power cannot simply be transferred to another individual in the way that traditional or rational authority can be transferred through appointment or election. The continuity of a group can be assured only if there is some way in which a successor or representative can be designated. This necessarily involves a dilution or routinisation of the original charisma and, therefore, a change in its character. The routinisation of charisma involves 'a step from autonomous leadership based on the power of personal charisma toward legitimacy derived from the authority of a "source"' (1914: 1124). Personal attachment to the successor is justified on the grounds that the charismatic leader has designated him or her as a worthy inheritor of the gift, but this involves a subtle shift from recognition of a personal gift by the followers to their acceptance of a leader who is appointed through some accepted procedure. Thus, when 'exposed to the conditions of everyday life, it loses its charismatic quality and becomes merely traditional authority' (1914: 1121–2): 'As soon as charismatic domination loses its personal foundation and the acutely emotional faith which disfranchises it from the traditional mold of everyday life, its alliance with tradition is the most obvious and often the only alternative' (1914: 1122). Weber notes that 'In such an alliance the essence of charisma appears to be definitely abandoned' (1914: 1122).

The recognition or acknowledgement of a successor by the followers may also be the first step towards the introduction of an electoral principle of succession with established procedural rules. Personal recognition and acclamation of a gifted leader becomes the institutionalised approval of a successor. Once this 'rationalisation of organisational techniques' begins, Weber argued, charisma may become allied with rational authority. In this alliance, charisma is weakened and may eventually disappear: 'It is the fate of charisma to recede before the powers of tradition or of rational association after it has entered the permanent structures of social action' (1914: 1148).

Wherever routinisation occurs, however, Weber recognised the possibility that some kind of impersonal or depersonalised charisma might become a normal feature of power relations. This occurs, for example, when leaders are believed to have a degree of charisma because of the specific positions that they occupy. In traditional structures, for example, charisma may sometimes be seen as transferable by inheritance through a blood lineage, and Weber termed this 'hereditary charisma' (1914: 1135–8). In such a situation, leaders may be seen as charismatic because they are descended from an original charismatic leader or because they are members of the same family. The charisma is seen as something that is associated with inheritable general characteristics and, therefore, as something that permeates, to a greater or lesser degree, a whole kinship group. Royal power, for example, is often justified in this way.

Another form of depersonalised charisma that Weber identified is what he called 'office charisma', which occurs where charisma is seen as an attribute of a formal position of traditional or bureaucratic authority (1914: 1139–41). It may be believed, for example, that any occupant of a particular position must have certain personal qualities, and such an occupant may, therefore, be able to demand a degree of personal allegiance. Charisma may, thus, be ascribed to anyone who happens to be a king or a bishop, however their position was obtained. Such individuals have a personal normative power (Etzioni 1961) over and above their formal powers of command.

Weber saw charismatic leadership as being a relatively marginal or short-lived phenomenon in modern societies, where the conditions for its maintenance did not always exist. While small religious sects and cults may be able to operate through charismatic leadership, charismatic political movements tend gradually to develop into the more or less bureaucratic parties that compete for power in modern states (1914: 1132). However, charisma has been more persistent than he thought. Traditional or rational structures of authority have frequently seen the 'eruption' of charisma and its maintenance for a time. Charismatic leaders may arise in political parties and endeavour to break the hold of party bureaucrats. They may build a faction of devoted followers and use this to build a larger body of popular support that will give them an independent power base within the party apparatus. Indeed, it has been suggested that those who feel 'disenchanted' and alienated from the power structures of the modern world may be very susceptible to the appeal of such charismatic leaders (Lindholm 1990: 47–9; see also Bryman 1992). Examples of this form of modern charismatic politics are Gladstone's Home Rule campaign and Roosevelt's 1912 election campaign (both cited by Weber), and, more recently, the leadership exercised by Churchill during the Second World War and Thatcher in the 1980s. Adolf Hitler is, perhaps, the most extreme example of the rise of charismatic leadership within a rationalised structure of power.

Charismatic leadership can also occur in the large organisations that dominate modern economies. Authority figures may have additional charismatic power if people feel especially attracted to them because of their perceived personal abilities or image. The holder of a formal position of command, for example, may be believed to possess certain extraordinary abilities that give him or her powers over and above those that are tied to the formal position itself. A 'visionary' or 'inspirational' manager, for example, may be able to motivate subordinates to tasks – seen as reflecting his or her personal mission – that are over and above the ordinary day-to-day routines of office work (Bryman 1992).

8
Coda

In this book I have been able only to scratch the surface of the complex phenomenon of power. I have concentrated on showing that there is a core idea to the concept of power and that this can be traced from its elementary forms to the more complex patterns of domination that are found in states, economic structures, and associations of all kinds. I have shown the forms of counteraction that occur in relation to such domination, and I have examined the more informally structured patterns of interpersonal power that permeate the formal structures of domination and counteraction.

To make this task realistic in such a short book, I have concentrated on delineating the broad characteristics of these various aspects of power. I have not applied these ideas in a systematic and comparative study of the actual patterns of power found in the world today. Instead, I have sought to show the relevance of the theoretical debates through using historical and contemporary data as illustrations of the various facets of power. I have highlighted the key studies and their methodological approaches, and I have drawn on the data from these studies and from other critical and supportive work. I hope that this incomplete task will encourage readers to pursue the debates and their empirical implications in the many detailed studies of power carried out in various contemporary societies.

My starting point was the claim that, behind all the political and conceptual disputes, a core idea of power could be identified. Power is the production of causal effects, and in the social world this is the intentional use of an agent's causal powers to affect the conduct of others in the social relations that connect them together. Using the terms 'principal' and 'subaltern' to refer to the two sides that there are in any power relation, I explored both the mainstream and the second-stream implementations of this core idea. From here I was able to set out the elementary forms of social power: corrective influence that operates through punishments and rewards, and persuasive influence that operates through the offering and accepting of reasons for action. These elementary forms of power give rise to relations of force, manipulation, signification, and legitimation, and they are the building blocks for the developed forms of domination and counteraction.

In the sphere of domination I followed Pareto in highlighting the coercion exercised by the 'lions' and the inducement exercised by the 'foxes'. Alongside these, however, I recognised the expertise of the 'owls' and the command of the 'bears'. Coercion and inducement are organised into structures of constraint, while expertise and command are organised into structures of authority. Constraint and authority, I showed, are inextricably linked in concrete structures of domination and can be separated only for analytical purposes. These distinctions allowed me to pursue the question of domination through more detailed considerations of command (chapter 2), constraint (chapter 4), and expertise (chapter 5). My argument was, in many respects, a cumulative one. The discussion of command, for example, was presupposed when I discussed constraint, and I looked at the complex articulations through which these can be combined into structures of hegemony. My aim in developing the argument in this way was to show the analytical distinctions that have to be made, but then to show that they derive their real value from their combination in particular concrete cases. They are ideal types that rarely exist in anything approaching their pure forms.

The two forms of counteraction that I considered were pressure (chapter 3) and protest (chapter 6). Pressure is that form of counteraction that arises within an institutionalised structure of domination and that is accorded a degree of legitimacy; it is the recognised and established counterpart to authority. Protest, on the other hand, is counteraction that occurs outside the formal institutions of power and that poses a challenge to these very structures. These are, again, analytical distinctions that are often difficult to disentangle in concrete situations. Protest groups may achieve some of their goals and accommodate themselves to the established framework of power, transforming themselves into pressure groups; and pressure groups may be frustrated in their actions and mount progressively more confrontational protests.

Any comprehensive study of power must combine these various facets of domination and counteraction into a single framework, but even this cannot tell the whole story. Alongside these formal structures of power, and permeating them at every point, are the patterns of interpersonal power that I considered in chapter 7. These power relations are those of face-to-face and similar encounters, where power depends on personal attributes and characteristics as much as it does on office-holding or formal resources. In focusing on gendered patterns if patriarchal power – the key exemplar of interpersonal power – I showed that these relations of power have their focus in the family household and the private sphere of intimacy and sexuality. I argued, however, that patriarchal power permeates the public sphere as well as the private and that it is not possible to consider domination and counteraction in the public sphere without also recognising the impact of interpersonal power. The gendered regimes of recruitment to positions of command that I considered in chapter 2, for example, are the results of patriarchal patterns of power that shape the ways in which formal powers of command can be exercised.

Notes

Chapter 1 Patterns of Power

1 The discussion of these matters in Wrong (1979) is a revision of a much earlier and widely discussed statement (Wrong 1967–8).

2 Hegel saw power relations as occurring between a 'master' and a 'slave', but this implies a far too one-sided view of power. The terms 'principal' and 'subaltern' allow for more variation in the forms taken by asymmetrical power relations. The term 'subaltern' derives from Gramsci's (1926–37: 52) description of subordinate classes.

3 This French distinction between '*pouvoir*' and '*puissance*', recognised in other Latin-based languages, is analytically important, though English uses the single word 'power' to refer to both ideas.

4 See also various other essays by Parsons on politics and power in his (1969) compilation.

5 Foucault's writings are tantalisingly cryptic and – it has to be said – calculatedly ignorant of what most other writers have actually said about power. However Foucault has been enormously important in highlighting a number of neglected questions in the mainstream.

6 Persuasion may occur alongside, in isolation, or in conjunction with force or manipulation. The advertising industry's reliance on 'hidden persuaders', for example, can be seen as combining both persuasion and manipulation (Packard 1957; Wrong 1979: 32–4).

7   Wrong (1979) has called this mode of power simply 'persuasion', but he notes that it has to be distinguished from forms of persuasion in which no element of power exists. Wartenberg (1990) calls it 'influence', and he, too, notes the need to distinguish influential persuasion from 'rational persuasion' in which no power arises. To make this point clear and explicit, I prefer to combine Wrong's and Wartenberg's views into the single term 'persuasive influence'. The attempt to develop a satisfactory distinction between persuasive influence and persuasion that operates through free rational discussion is central to Habermas's (1970a; 1970b) idea of the ideal speech situation.

8   Corrective influence is a mechanism that operates in and through relational structures, while persuasive influence operates through institutional structures. For this distinction see López and Scott (2000).

9   In such an extreme situation, the agent's freedom of choice may approach the purely nominal freedom to choose that existentialists have seen as an inescapable feature of the human condition: but it is a choice, nevertheless.

10   Wrong (1979) refers to this form of power as 'competence' rather than 'expertise'.

11   Poggi (2000: 123–4) equates domination by virtue of authority with political domination and domination by virtue of a constellation of interests with economic domination. As I have suggested, this view does not adequately reflect the diversity of the various forms of domination.

Chapter 2   Command and Sovereign Power

1   See the useful discussion of some of these characteristics in Pierson (1996).

2   The constitution need not, of course, be a written one.

3   Many studies have considered church elites, 'media elites', and 'university elites' along with the state elite, but it is important to keep them separate. Political party elites and the leaders of pressure groups and voluntary associations, similarly, are not parts of the state, and their main significance is in relation to their exercise of pressure. I will look at these organisations in chapter 4.

4   I will return to Mills' discussion of the corporate rich in a later section of this chapter.

5   The concept of a regime of recruitment is a generalisation of the idea of the 'gender regime' that was introduced by Connell (1987; 1990).

6　Putnam (1976: 33) describes what he calls a 'law of increasing disproportion'. According to this 'law', disproportionality in recruitment increases with the level of command. Putnam suggests that this 'law' – in fact, an empirical generalisation – applies to gender and ethnicity, but he illustrates it only in relation to data on class.

7　Holdaway (1983), for example, has documented the existence of a masculine 'cop culture' that permeates the police force from top to bottom.

8　This argument draws on the lengthier discussion in Scott (1997).

9　Some of the key studies of political and economic elites using these methods can be found in Scott (1990a).

Chapter 3　Pressure and Policy Formation

1　I will not give so much attention to the broader functionalist and consensus arguments with which it is often associated. A broader account of pluralism can be found in Alford and Friedland (1985: part 1).

2　In addition, as I show in chapter 5, policy compromises result from external constraints on a government's ability to deliver particular outcomes.

3　Dahl actually drew much stronger conclusions than this, believing that power was essentially pluralistic. There is a limitation in the scope of the power available to individual actors, and their total power, he argues, reflects the non-combinable nature of power resources. Wealth, positions of authority, and social honour, for example, are distinct sources of power that have no one-to-one relationship with each other. It is possible to achieve certain things with wealth and other things with authority, but they are rarely interchangeable.

4　Thus, Newton (1975: 18) has correctly pointed to the need to speak of an 'institutionalisation of bias' as well as its subsequent mobilisation.

5　This discussion draws on the listing of functions given in Domhoff (1979: 120–1).

6　Interlock studies and policy network studies both use social network analysis, but they do so differently. The networks explored by policy network analysts are one-dimensional power networks (the exercise of power); the networks investigated in positional studies are structures of command (the holding of power). Surprisingly, analysts of policy networks have not, for the most part, used techniques of network analysis to explore the sociometric structure of policy networks. They have, instead, used the idea in a more impressionistic way. For a discussion of social network analysis see Scott (2000b).

Chapter 4   Constraint and Hegemony

1   Previously (Scott 1997) I have followed the lead of Mintz and Schwartz (1985) and have termed this 'financial hegemony'. For reasons set out later in this chapter, I now feel that it may be useful to distinguish between this kind of constraint and hegemony proper.

2   The distinction that Waltz (1979) makes between hierarchy and anarchy exactly parallels the distinction that Williamson (1975) made between hierarchy and market in national economies.

3   The standard narrative account can be found in Keohane (1984: chapters 9 and 10). See also Brown (1997).

4   See the useful summary of the related arguments of Bridges and Bock in Barrow (1993).

Chapter 5   Discipline and Expertise

1   Unsurprisingly, perhaps, Foucault's discussion of power has re-discovered many ideas that had, in fact, been central to the works of those that he criticised or rejected.

2   It is, of course, significant that the word 'discipline' also describes systematic bodies of knowledge such as scientific disciplines.

3   Foucault's concept of the carceral organisation seems to play on a similarity of sound and spelling between two unrelated words: the body as a 'carcass' and its confinement as 'incarceration'.

4   As has often been remarked, Foucault's discussion of carceral organisations reiterates many points made by Goffman (1961) in his discussion of 'total institutions'.

5   It is, perhaps, worth noting the etymological association of 'discipline' with 'discipleship'.

6   See the larger explorations of this view in arguments about the 'knowledge society' in Bell (1973) and Wilensky (1967). Such views were restated on a different basis in Lyotard (1979).

7   Gouldner used the word 'discipline' rather than 'command'. In view of Foucault's popularisation of the word 'discipline'

in a slightly different sense, I have altered Gouldner's terminology.

8 Cf. Foucault on the socialisation dimension of productive power.

9 Jackson and Carter (1998: 55) argue that line managers have increasingly become experts to the extent that management and business studies and the study of human resources management provide them with monopoly knowledge of the techniques of governmentality that allow them to discipline workers into obedience.

Chapter 6   Protest and Collective Mobilisation

1 Melucci makes this equation of protest with social movement in an explicit attempt to make the term 'social movement' self-destruct.

2 Smelser's idea of the 'generalised beliefs' that connected social strains to their supposed solution was a direct counterpart to Mosca's idea of the 'political formula' that masked the irrational interests driving political action.

3 The book by Tilly et al. (1975) contains studies of France, Italy, and Germany by the three authors, together with some comparative analysis. The study of France was carried out by Charles Tilly.

4 Calvert (1992) makes the important point that a revolution in the sense that I have defined it differs from mere long-term processes of change, however radical the transformation may be. The 'industrial revolution' and the 'neolithic revolution', for example, are not true revolutions. A revolution occurs through deliberate contention in relation to a programme and through a key event, or sequence of events, that overthrow an established leadership.

5 The WTO was set up in 1995 to replace the earlier General Agreement on Tariffs and Trade (GATT).

Chapter 7   Interpersonal Power

1 In addition to the bases of power listed here, French and Raven point to the importance of legitimacy and expertise as bases of power in relations of domination.

2 Feminist discussions of patriarchy have often taken Engels' account as their starting point. For Engels, however, 'patriarchy' referred to precisely the same type of family structure that Weber termed 'patriarchalism'.

3 Referring to their socialisation, Bartky notes that many women feel impelled to remove their body hair, but that 'noone is marched off for electrolysis at gunpoint' (Bartky 1988: 38).

4 Foucault's own account of the body often ignores the resistance that his general account of power requires, and he tends towards a view of the body as a totally passive and malleable 'docile body'.

5 Lindholm (1990) notes that Weber failed to discuss the social–psychological basis of charismatic leadership, and he points to the contribution that could have been made if Weber had drawn on the related arguments of Taine and Le Bon (1895) to provide this.

Bibliography

All books and articles are cited by date of first publication in the original language, or date of writing in the case of posthumous sources. If the date of the edition used differs from the citation date, it is given at the end of the reference.

Abbott, A. 1988. *The System of Professions: An Essay on the Division of Expert Labour*. Chicago: University of Chicago Press.

Abercrombie, N., B. Turner, and S. Hill. 1979. *The Dominant Ideology Thesis*. London: George Allen and Unwin.

Abercrombie, N., B. Turner, and S. Hill. 1986. *Sovereign Individuals of Capitalism*. London: George Allen and Unwin.

Alford, R. R. and R. Friedland. 1985. *Powers of Theory*. Cambridge: Cambridge University Press.

Allen, M. P. 1978. Conflict and change within the corporate elite. *Sociological Quarterly*, 19.

Allen, M. P. 1987. *The Founding Fortunes: A New Anatomy of the Super-rich Families in America*. New York: E. P. Dutton.

Almond, G. and S. Verba. 1963. *Civic Culture*. Princeton: Princeton University Press.

Althusser, L. 1971. *Lenin and Philosophy and Other Essays*. London: New Left Books.

Anderson, P. 1976. The antinomies of Antonio Gramsci. *New Left Review*, 100.

Arendt, H. 1959. *The Human Condition*. New York: Anchor Books.

Arendt, H. 1970. *On Violence*. Harmondsworth: Allen Lane, The Penguin Press.

Arrighi, G., T. C. Hopkins, and I. Wallerstein. 1989. *Antisystemic Movements*. London: Verso.

Arrow, K. 1951. *Social Choice and Individual Values*. New Haven: Yale University Press.

Ash, R. 1972. *Social Movements in America*. Chicago: Markham.

Bachrach, P. and M. S. Baratz. 1962. The two faces of power. In *Power*, vol. 2. Edited by J. Scott. London: Routledge, 1994.

Bachrach, P. and M. S. Baratz. 1963. Decisions and nondecisions: An analytical framework. In *Power*, vol. 2. Edited by J. Scott. London: Routledge, 1994.

Bachrach, P. and M. S. Baratz. 1970. *Power and Poverty*. New York: Oxford University Press.

Ball, T. 1975. Models of power: Past and present. *Journal of the History of the Behavioural Sciences*, 11.

Ball, T. 1976. Power, causation and explanation. *Polity*, 8.

Barnes, S. B. 1988. *The Nature of Power*. Cambridge: Polity.

Barrett, M. 1980. *Women's Oppression Today*. London: Verso.

Barrett, M. 1988. Introduction. In *Women's Oppression Today*, rev. edn. Edited by M. Barrett. London: Verso.

Barrett, M. and M. McIntosh. 1982. *The Anti-social Family*. London: Verso.

Barrow, C. W. 1993. *Critical Theories of the State*. Madison: University of Wisconsin Press.

Bartky, S. 1988. Foucault, femininity and the modernisation of patriarchal power. In *Feminism and Foucault: Reflections on Resistance*. Edited by I. Diamond and L. Quinby. Boston: Northeastern University Press.

Bates, T. R. 1975. Gramsci and the theory of hegemony. *Journal of the History of Ideas*, 36.

Baudrillard, J. 1981. *Simulations*. New York: Semiotext(e), 1983.

Bavelas, A. 1950. Common patterns in task-oriented groups. In *Group Dynamics: Research and Theory*, 3rd edn. Edited by D. Cartwright and A. Zander. London: Tavistock, 1968.

Beck, U. 1986. *Risk Society: Towards a New Modernity*. London: Sage, 1992.

Beetham, D. 1991. *The Legitimation of Power*. Basingstoke: Macmillan.

Bell, D. 1961. *The End of Ideology*. New York: Collier-Macmillan.

Bell, D. 1973. *The Coming of Post-industrial Society*. New York: Basic Books.

Bentley, A. F. 1908. *The Process of Government: A Study of Social Pressure*. New Brunswick: Transaction Publishers.

Benton, T. 1981. Objective interests and the sociology of power. In *Power*, vol. 2. Edited by J. Scott. London: Routledge, 1994.

Berle, A. A. and G. C. Means. 1932. *The Modern Corporation and Private Property*. London: Macmillan.

Bland, L. 1979. The domain of the sexual: A response. *Screen Education*, 39.

Blood, R. and D. M. Wolfe. 1960. *Husbands and Wives*. New York: Free Press.

Bottomore, T. and R. J. Brym (eds). 1989. *The Capitalist Class*. Hemel Hempstead: Harvester Wheatsheaf.

Bourdieu, P. 1979. *Distinction: A Social Critique of the Judgement of Taste*. London: Routledge, 1984.

Bourdieu, P. and J. Passeron. 1970. *Reproduction in Economy and Society*. London: Sage, 1990.

Boyd, D. 1973. *Elites and Their Education*. Windsor: National Foundation for Educational Research.

Brannen, J. and P. Moss. 1991. *Managing Mothers*. London: Unwin Hyman.

Brint, S. 1994. *In an Age of Experts*. Princeton: Princeton University Press.

Brown, C. 1997. *Understanding International Relations*. New York: St Martin's Press.

Bryman, A. 1992. *Charisma and Leadership in Organisations*. London: Sage.

Buchanan, J. 1975. *The Limits of Liberty*. Chicago: Chicago University Press.

Buchanan, J. M. and G. Tullock. 1962. *The Calculus of Consent*. Ann Arbor: University of Michigan Press.

Bull, H. 1977. *The Anarchical Society*. London: Macmillan.

Burnham, J. 1943. *The Machiavellians*. New York: John Day.

Butler, J. 1990. *Gender Trouble*. London: Routledge.

Calvert, P. 1992. *Revolution and Counter-revolution*. Buckingham: Open University Press.

Carmichael, S. and C. Hamilton. 1967. *Black Power*. New York: Random House.

Castells, M. 1996. *The Rise of the Network Society, Volume 1 of The Information Age: Economy, Society and Culture*. Oxford: Blackwell.

Chandler, A. D. 1990. *Scale and Scope*. Cambridge, Mass.: The Belknap Press of Harvard University Press.

Chase-Dunn, C. and B. Podobnik. 1999. The next world war: World-system cycles and trends. In *The Future of Global Conflict*. Edited by V. Bornschier and C. Chase-Dunn. Beverly Hills: Sage.

Clegg, S. R. 1989. *Frameworks of Power*. London: Sage.

Cole, G. D. H. 1920. *Social Theory*. London: Methuen.

Connell, R. W. 1987. *Gender and Power.* Cambridge: Polity.

Connell, R. W. 1990. The state, gender and sexual politics. In *Power/Gender: Social Relations in Theory and Practice.* Edited by H. L. Radtke and H. J. Stam. London: Sage, 1994.

Cook, K. S., R. M. Emerson, M. R. Gillmore, and T. Yamagishi. 1983. The distribution of power in exchange networks: Theory and experimental results. In *Power*, vol. 2. Edited by J. Scott. London: Routledge, 1994.

Crenson, M. A. 1971. *The Un-politics of Air Pollution: A Study of Nondecision-making in the Cities.* Baltimore: The Johns Hopkins Press.

Dahl, R. A. 1957. The concept of power. In *Power*, vol. 2. Edited by J. Scott. London: Routledge, 1994.

Dahl, R. A. 1968. Power as the control of behaviour. In *Power*. Edited by S. Lukes. Oxford: Oxford University Press, 1986.

Dahl, R. A. 1971. *Polyarchy: Participation and Opposition.* New Haven: Yale University Press.

Dandecker, C. 1990. *Surveillance, Power and Modernity.* Cambridge: Polity.

de Jouvenel, B. 1945. *Power: The Natural History of Its Growth.* London: Hutchinson, 1948.

Dean, H. 1999. *Governmentality.* London: Sage.

Della Porta, D. and M. Diani. 1999. *Social Movements.* Oxford: Blackwell.

Delphy, C. 1977. *The Main Enemy.* London: Women's Research and Resources Centre.

Diani, M. 1992. The concept of social movement. *Sociological Review*, 40.

Domhoff, G. W. 1967. *Who Rules America?* Englewood Cliffs: Prentice Hall.

Domhoff, G. W. 1971. *The Higher Circles: The Governing Class in America.* New York: Vintage Books.

Domhoff, G. W. 1974. *The Bohemian Groves.* New York: Harper and Row.

Domhoff, G. W. 1979. *The Powers That Be: Processes of Ruling Class Domination in America.* New York: Vintage.

Domhoff, G. W. (ed.) 1980. *Power Structure Research.* Beverly Hills: Sage.

Domhoff, G. W. 1998. *Who Rules America? Power and Politics in the Year 2000.* Mountain View: Mayfield Publishing.

Dowding, K. 1996. *Power.* Buckingham: Open University Press.

Downs, A. 1957. *An Economic Theory of Democracy.* New York: Harper and Brothers.

Durkheim, E. 1895. *The Rules of the Sociological Method*. London: Macmillan, 1982.

Durkheim, E. 1917. *Professional Ethics and Civic Morals*. London: Routledge and Kegan Paul, 1957.

Eckstein, H. 1961. *A Theory of Stable Democracy*. Princeton, NJ: Woodrow Wilson School.

Eichler, M. 1981. Power, dependence, love, and the sexual division of labour. *Women's Studies International Quarterly*, 4.

Elster, J. 1989. *The Cement of Society*. Cambridge: Cambridge University Press.

Emerson, R. M. 1962. Power-dependence relations. In *Power*, vol. 2. Edited by J. Scott. London: Routledge, 1994.

Esland, G. 1980. Professions and professionalism. In *The Politics of Work and Occupations*. Edited by G. Esland and G. Salaman. Milton Keynes: Open University Press.

Etzioni, A. 1961. *A Comparative Analysis of Complex Organizations: On Power, Involvement, and their Correlates*. New York: Free Press.

Etzioni, A. 1964. *Modern Organizations*. Englewood Cliffs: Prentice Hall.

Etzioni, A. 1969. *The Semi-professions and Their Organization*. New York: Free Press.

Eyerman, R. and A. Jamison. 1991. *Social Movements*. Cambridge: Polity.

Festinger, L. 1957. *A Theory of Cognitive Dissonance*. London: Tavistock, 1962.

Firestone, S. 1971. *The Dialectic of Sex*. London: Jonathan Cape.

Foucault, M. 1961. *Madness and Civilization*. New York: Vintage Books, 1973.

Foucault, M. 1963. *The Birth of the Clinic*. New York: Vintage Books, 1975.

Foucault, M. 1975. *Discipline and Punish*. London: Allen Lane, 1977.

Foucault, M. 1976. *An Introduction. The History of Sexuality, Volume 1*. New York: Vintage Books, 1980.

Foucault, M. 1978. Governmentality. In *The Foucault Effect: Studies in Governmentality*. Edited by G. Burchell, C. Gordon, and P. Miller. London: Harvester Wheatsheaf, 1991.

Foucault, M. 1982. The subject and power. In *Power*, vol. 1. Edited by J. Scott. London: Routledge, 1994.

Foucault, M. 1984a. *The Use of Pleasure. The History of Sexuality, Volume 2*. New York: Vintage Books, 1986.

Foucault, M. 1984b. *The Care of the Self. The History of Sexuality, Volume 3*. New York: Vintage Books, 1988.

Freidkin, N. 1998. *A Structural Theory of Social Influence.* Cambridge: Cambridge University Press.

Freidson, E. 1970a. *The Profession of Medicine.* New York: Dodd Mead.

Freidson, E. 1970b. *Professional Dominance.* Chicago: Aldine.

Freidson, E. 1973. Professions and the occupational principle. In *Professionalism Reborn.* Cambridge: Polity, 1994.

Freidson, E. 1993. How dominant are the professions? In *Professionalism Reborn.* Cambridge: Polity, 1994.

French, J. R. P. 1956. A formal theory of social power. *Psychological Review*, 63.

French, J. R. P. and B. Raven. 1959. The bases of social power. In *Studies in Social Power.* Edited by D. Cartwright. Ann Arbor: University of Michigan Press.

Friedrich, C. J. 1937. *Constitutional Government and Democracy.* Waltham: Blaisdell Publishing, 1968.

Gamarnikow, E. 1978. Sexual division of labour: The case of nursing. In *Feminism and Materialism.* Edited by A. Kuhn and A.-M. Wolpe. London: Routledge and Kegan Paul.

Gamson, W. A. 1975. *The Strategy of Protest.* Homewood, Ill.: Dorsey Press.

Gellner, E. 1988. *Plough, Sword, and Book: The Structure of Human History.* London: Collins.

Gerlach, M. L. 1992. *Alliance Capitalism: The Social Organisation of Japanese Business.* Berkeley: University of California Press.

Giddens, A. 1973. Elites in the British class structure. In *The Sociology of Elites*, vol. 1. Edited by J. Scott. Cheltenham: Edward Elgar, 1990.

Giddens, A. 1976. *New Rules of the Sociological Method.* London: Hutchinson.

Giddens, A. 1979. *Central Problems in Social Theory.* London: Macmillan.

Giddens, A. 1981. *A Contemporary Critique of Historical Materialism.* London: Macmillan.

Giddens, A. 1982. Action, structure, power. In *Profiles and Critiques in Social Theory.* Edited by A. Giddens. London: Macmillan.

Giddens, A. 1984. *The Constitution of Society.* Cambridge: Polity.

Giddens, A. 1985. *The Nation State and Violence, Volume 2 of A Contemporary Critique of Historical Materialism.* Cambridge: Polity.

Giddens, A. 1989. *The Consequences of Modernity.* Cambridge: Polity.

Giddens, A. 1991. *Modernity and Self-identity.* Cambridge: Polity.

Glasberg, D. S. 1989. *The Power of Collective Purse Strings: The Effects of Bank Hegemony on Corporations and the State.* Berkeley: University of California Press.

Goffman, E. 1959. *The Presentation of Self in Everyday Life.* Harmondsworth: Penguin.

Goffman, E. 1961. *Asylums: Essays on the Social Situation of Mental Patients and Other Inmates.* New York: Doubleday.

Goldthorpe, J. H. 1980. *Social Mobility and Class Structure.* Oxford: Clarendon Press.

Gouldner, A. 1954a. *Patterns of Industrial Bureaucracy.* New York: Free Press.

Gouldner, A. 1954b. *Wildcat Strike.* New York: Harper and Row.

Gouldner, A. 1957. Cosmopolitans and locals. *Administrative Science Quarterly*, 2.

Gramsci, A. 1926–37. *Selections from the Prison Notebooks of Antonio Gramsci.* London: Lawrence and Wishart, 1971.

Grant, W. 1987. *Business and Politics in Britain.* London: Macmillan.

Grant, W. and D. Marsh. 1977. *The Confederation of British Industry.* London: Hodder and Stoughton.

Gusfield. 1963. *Symbolic Crusade.* Urbana: University of Illinois Press.

Guttsman, W. L. 1963. *The British Political Elite.* London: MacGibbon and Kee.

Habermas, J. 1962. *The Structural Transformation of the Public Sphere.* Cambridge, Mass.: MIT Press, 1989.

Habermas, J. 1970a. On systematically distorted communication. *Inquiry*, 13.

Habermas, J. 1970b. Towards a theory of communicative competence. In *Recent Sociology*, no. 2. Edited by H. P. Dreitzel. New York: Macmillan.

Habermas, J. 1973. *Legitimation Crisis.* London: Heinemann, 1976.

Habermas, J. 1981a. *The Theory of Communicative Action, Volume One: Reason and the Rationalization of Society.* Cambridge: Polity, 1984.

Habermas, J. 1981b. *The Theory of Communicative Action, Volume Two: The Critique of Functionalist Reason.* Cambridge: Polity, 1987.

Halliday, F. 1983. *The Making of the Second Cold War.* London: Verso.

Halliday, F. 1999. *Revolution and World Politics.* Basingstoke: Macmillan.

Hartsock, N. 1983. *Money, Sex and Power: Toward a Feminist Historical Materialism*. Boston: Northeastern University Press.

Haugaard, M. 1997. *The Constitution of Power*. Manchester: Manchester University Press.

Held, D. 1987. *Models of Democracy*. Cambridge: Polity.

Held, D. 1989. *Political Theory and the Modern State*. Cambridge: Polity.

Herman, E. O. 1981. *Corporate Control, Corporate Power*. New York: Oxford University Press.

Hilferding, R. 1910. *Finance Capital*. London: Routledge and Kegan Paul, 1981.

Hindess, B. 1996. *Discourses of Power: From Hobbes to Foucault*. Oxford: Blackwell.

Hochschild, A. R. 1983. *The Managed Heart: Commercialization of Human Feeling*. Berkeley: University of California Press.

Hogwood, B. 1987. *From Crisis to Complacency*. Oxford: Oxford University Press.

Holdaway, S. 1983. *Inside the British Police*. Oxford: Blackwell.

Holloway, W. 1994. Separation, integration and difference: Contradiction in a gender regime. In *Power/Gender: Social Relations in Theory and Practice*. Edited by H. L. Radtke and H. J. Stam. London: Sage.

Hopkins, T. and I. Wallerstein. 1982. *World Systems Analysis*. Beverly Hills: Sage.

Hunter, F. 1953. *Community Power Structure*. Chapel Hill: University of North Carolina Press.

Ingham, G. K. 1984. *Capitalism Divided?* London: Macmillan.

Inkeles, A. and D. Smith. 1974. *Becoming Modern*. Cambridge, Mass.: Harvard University Press.

Isaac, J. C. 1987. *Power and Marxist Theory: A Realist View*. Ithaca: Cornell University Press.

Isaac, J. C. 1992. Beyond the three faces of power: A realist critique. In *Rethinking Power*. Edited by T. Wartenberg. Albany: State University of New York Press.

Jackson, N. and P. Carter. 1998. Labour as dressage. In *Foucault, Management and Organisation Theory*. Edited by A. McKinlay and K. Starkey. London: Sage.

Jessop, R. 1972. *Social Order, Reform and Revolution*. London: Macmillan.

Johnson, T. 1972. *Professions and Power*. London: Macmillan.

Johnson, T. 1993. Expertise and the state. In *Foucault's New Domains*. Edited by M. Gane and T. Johnson. London: Routledge.

Kaplan, M. 1957. *System and Process in International Politics*. New York: Wiley.

Keck, M. E. and K. Sikkink. 1998. *Activists Beyond Borders: Advocacy Networks in International Politics*. Ithaca: Cornell University Press.

Kennedy, P. 1987. *The Rise and Fall of the Great Powers, 1500–2000*. New York: Random House.

Keohane, R. O. 1984. *After Hegemony: Cooperation and Discord in the World Political Economy*. Princeton: Princeton University Press.

Keohane, R. O. and J. S. Nye (eds). 1971. *Transnational Relations and World Politics*. Cambridge, Mass.: Harvard University Press.

Kerr, C., J. T. Dunlop, F. Harbison, and C. A. Myers. 1960. *Industrialism and Industrial Man*. Cambridge, Mass.: Harvard University Press.

Kriesi, H., R. Koopmans, J. W. Dyvendak, and M. G. Giugni. 1995. *New Social Movements in Western Europe*. London: UCL Press.

Landry, B. 1987. *The New Black Middle Class*. Berkeley: University of California Press.

Larson, M. 1977. *The Rise of Professionalism*. Berkeley: University of California Press.

Lash, S. and J. Urry. 1987. *The End of Organized Capitalism*. Cambridge: Polity.

Laski, H. J. 1917. *Studies in the Problem of Sovereignty*. New Haven: Yale University Press.

Laski, H. J. 1919. *Authority in the Modern State*. Hamdon, Conn.: Archon Books, 1968.

Lasswell, H. D. and A. Kaplan. 1950. *Power and Society*. New Haven: Yale University Press.

Laumann, E. O. and D. Knoke. 1989. Policy networks of the organisational state. In *Networks of Power*. Edited by R. Perrucci and H. R. Potter. New York: De Gruyter.

Layder, D. 1985. Power, structure and agency. *Journal for the Theory of Social Behaviour*, 15.

Le Bon, G. 1895. *The Crowd*. London: Ernest Benn, 1896.

Lindblom, C. E. 1977. *Politics and Markets: The World's Political–Economic Systems*. New York: Basic Books.

Lindholm, C. 1990. *Charisma*. Oxford: Blackwell.

Lippitt, R. 1952. The dynamics of power. *Human Relations*, 5.

Lipset, S. M. 1959. *Political Man*. London: Heinemann, 1960.

Lipset, S. M. 1963. *The First New Nation*. London: Heinemann, 1964.

Longstreth, F. 1979. The city, industry and the state. In *State and Economy in Contemporary Capitalism*. Edited by C. Crouch. London: Croom Helm.

López, J. and J. Scott. 2000. *Social Structure*. Buckingham: Open University Press.

Lukes, S. 1974. *Power: A Radical View*. London: Macmillan.

Lukes, S. 1977. Power and structure. In *Essays in Social Theory*. London: Macmillan.

Lukes, S. 1978. Power and authority. In *A History of Sociological Analysis*. Edited by T. B. Bottomore and R. A. Nisbet. London: Heinemann.

Lukes, S. 1986. Introduction. In *Power*. Edited by S. Lukes. Oxford: Oxford University Press.

Lynd, R. S. and H. M. Lynd. 1929. *Middletown*. New York: Harcourt Brace.

Lynd, R. S. and H. M. Lynd. 1937. *Middletown in Transition*. New York: Harcourt Brace.

Lyotard, J.-F. 1979. *The Postmodern Condition*. Manchester: Manchester University Press, 1984.

Machiavelli, N. 1513. *The Prince*. Oxford: Oxford University Press, 1984.

Macpherson, C. B. 1962. *The Political Theory of Possessive Individualism*. Oxford: Clarendon Press.

Mann, M. 1970. The social cohesion of liberal democracy. *American Sociological Review*, 35.

Mann, M. 1986a. A crisis in stratification theory. In *Gender and Stratification*. Edited by R. Crompton and M. Mann. Cambridge: Polity.

Mann, M. 1986b. *The Sources of Social Power*, vol. 1. Cambridge: Cambridge University Press.

Mannheim, K. 1947. *Freedom, Power and Democratic Planning*. London: Routledge and Kegan Paul, 1951.

McCarthy, J. D. and M. N. Zald. 1977. Resource mobilization and social movements: A partial theory. *American Journal of Sociology*, 82.

McLennan, G. 1995. *Pluralism*. Buckingham: Open University Press.

McNay, L. 1992. *Foucault and Feminism: Power, Gender and the Self*. Cambridge: Polity.

Meisel, J. H. 1958. *The Myth of the Ruling Class*. Ann Arbor: Michigan University Press.

Melucci, A. 1996. *Challenging Codes: Collective Action in the Information Age*. Cambridge: Cambridge University Press.

Michels, R. 1911. *Political Parties*. New York: Herst's International Library, 1915.

Middleton, C. 1974. Sexual inequality and stratification theory. In *The Social Analysis of Class Structure*. Edited by F. Parkin. London: Tavistock.

Miliband, R. 1969. *The State in Capitalist Society*. London: Weidenfeld and Nicolson.

Miliband, R. 1982. *Capitalist Democracy in Britain*. Oxford: Oxford University Press.

Millet, K. 1970. *Sexual Politics*. New York: Doubleday.

Mills, C. W. 1956. *The Power Elite*. New York: Oxford University Press.

Mintz, B. and M. Schwartz. 1985. *The Power Structure of American Business*. Chicago: Chicago University Press.

Mintz, B. and M. Schwartz. 1986. Capital flows and the process of financial hegemony. *Theory and Society*, 15.

Mizruchi, M. S. 1982. *The American Corporate Network, 1900–1974*. London: Sage.

Morgenthau, H. J. 1948. *Politics Among Nations: The Struggle for Power and Peace*. New York: Alfred P. Knopf.

Morris, L. and Ruane, S. 1989. *Household Finance Management and the Labour Market*. Aldershot: Gower.

Morriss, P. 1987. *Power*. Manchester: Manchester University Press.

Mosca, G. 1896. *Elementi di Scienza Politica*, first edition. In *The Ruling Class*. New York: McGraw Hill, 1939.

Mulholland, K. 1994. Female kin and male capitalists: His dream and my money. *Work, Employment and Society*, 8.

Murray, M. 1995. *The Law of the Father*. London: Routledge.

Newby, H. 1975. The deferential dialectic. *Comparative Studies in Society and History*, 17.

Newton, K. 1975. Community politics and decision-making: The American experience and its lessons. In *Essays on the Study of Urban Politics*. London: Croom Helm.

Norris, P. and J. Lovenduski. 1995. *Political Recruitment*. Cambridge: Cambridge University Press.

Oberschall, A. 1973. *Social Conflict and Social Movements*. Englewood Cliffs: Prentice-Hall.

O'Brien, R., A. M. Goetz, J. A. Scholte, and M. Williams. 2000. *Contesting Global Governance*. Cambridge: Cambridge University Press.

O'Connor, J. 1973. *The Fiscal Crisis of the State*. New York: St. Martin's Press.

Olson, M. 1965. *The Logic of Collective Action*. Cambridge, Mass.: Harvard University Press.

Oppenheimer, M. 1973. The proletarianization of the professional. In *Sociological Review Monograph*, 20.

Packard, V. 1957. *The Hidden Persuaders*. Harmondsworth: Penguin, 1960.

Pahl, J. 1980. Patterns of money management within marriage. *Journal of Social Policy*, 9.

Pahl, R. E. and J. Winkler. 1974. The economic elite: Theory and practice. In *Elites and Power in British Society*. Edited by P. Stanworth and A. Giddens. Cambridge: Cambridge University Press.

Pareto, V. 1916. *A Treatise on General Sociology* (4 vols bound as 2). Edited by A. Livingstone. New York: Dover, 1963.

Parkin, F. 1967. Working class Conservatives: A theory of political deviance. *British Journal of Sociology*, 18.

Parkin, F. 1971. *Class Inequality and Political Order*. London: McGibbon and Kee.

Parsons, T. 1939. The professions and social structure. In *Essays in Sociological Theory*, 2nd edn. New York: Free Press, 1954.

Parsons, T. 1940. The motivation of economic activity. In *Essays in Sociological Theory*, 2nd edn. New York: Free Press, 1954.

Parsons, T. 1963. On the concept of political power. *Proceedings of the American Philosophical Society*, 107.

Parsons, T. (ed.) 1969. *Politics and Social Structure*. New York: The Free Press.

Parsons, T. and A. Henderson. 1947. Introduction. In *The Theory of Social and Economic Organisation [Max Weber]*. Edited by T. Parsons and A. Henderson. New York: Free Press.

Pfeffer, J. 1981. *Power in Organizations*. Boston: Pitman.

Pierson, C. 1996. *The Modern State*. London: Routledge.

Poggi, G. 2000. *Forms of Power*. Cambridge: Polity.

Polsby, N. W. 1960. How to study community power: The pluralist alternative. In *Power*, vol. 2. Edited by J. Scott. London: Routledge, 1994.

Polsby, N. W. 1962. *Community Power and Political Theory*. New Haven: Yale University Press, 2nd edn, 1980.

Poulantzas, N. 1968. *Political Power and Social Classes*. London: New Left Books, 1973.

Poulantzas, N. 1969. The problem of the capitalist state. *New Left Review*, 58.

Putnam, R. D. 1973. *The Beliefs of Politicians: Ideology, Conflict and Democracy in Britain and Italy*. New Haven: Yale University Press.

Putnam, R. D. 1976. *The Comparative Study of Political Elites*. Englewood Cliffs: Prentice-Hall.

Puwar, N. 2000. Embodying the Body Politic. Ph.D. thesis, University of Essex.

Renner, K. 1953. *Wandlungen der Modernen Gesellshaft.* Vienna: Verlag der Wiener Volksbuchhandlung.

Rhodes, R. A. W. 1981. *Control and Power in Central–Local Government Relationships.* Farnborough: Gower.

Rhodes, R. A. W. and D. Marsh. 1992. Networks in British politics. In *Policy Networks in British Government.* Edited by D. Marsh and R. A. W. Rhodes. Oxford: Oxford University Press.

Rose, N. 1998. *Inventing Our Selves: Psychology, Power and Personhood.* Cambridge: Cambridge University Press.

Roy, W. G. 1997. *Socializing Capital: The Rise of the Large Industrial Corporation in America.* Princeton: Princeton University Press.

Rueschemeyer, D. 1983. Professional authority and the social control of expertise. In *The Sociology of the Professions.* Edited by R. Dingwall and P. Lewis. Basingstoke: Macmillan.

Runciman, W. G. 1989. *A Treatise on Social Theory,* vol. 1. Cambridge: Cambridge University Press.

Safilios Rothschild, C. 1976. A macro and micro examination of family power and love: An exchange model. *Journal of Marriage and the Family,* 38.

Savage, M. 1998. Discourse, surveillance and the career. In *Foucault, Management and Organization Theory.* Edited by A. McKinley and K. Starkey. London: Sage.

Schattschneider. 1960. *The Semi-sovereign People.* New York: Holt, Rinehart and Winston.

Schelling, T. 1960. *The Strategy of Conflict.* Cambridge, Mass.: Harvard University Press.

Schmitter, P. 1979. Still the century of corporatism. In *Trends Towards Corporatist Intermediation.* Edited by P. Schmitter and G. Lehmbruch. London: Sage.

Schumpeter, J. 1954. The crisis of the tax state. *International Economic Papers,* 15.

Scott, J. (ed.) 1990a. *The Sociology of Elites* (3 vols). Cheltenham: Edward Elgar Publishing.

Scott, J. 1990b. Corporate control and corporate rule: Britain in an international perspective. *British Journal of Sociology,* 41.

Scott, J. 1991a. Networks of corporate power: A comparative assessment. *Annual Review of Sociology,* 17.

Scott, J. 1991b. *Who Rules Britain?* Cambridge: Polity.

Scott, J. 1996. *Stratification and Power: Structures of Class, Status and Command.* Cambridge: Polity.

Scott, J. 1997. *Corporate Business and Capitalist Classes.* Oxford: Oxford University Press.

Scott, J. 2000a. Rational choice theory. In *Understanding Contemporary Society*. Edited by G. Browning, A. Halcli, and F. Webster. London: Sage.

Scott, J. 2000b. *Social Network Analysis*, 2nd edn. London: Sage.

Scott, J. and C. Griff. 1984. *Directors of Industry*. Cambridge: Polity.

Scott, J. C. 1990. *Domination and the Arts of Resistance*. New Haven: Yale University Press.

Scott, W. R. 1966. Professionals in bureaucracies: Areas of conflict. In *Professionalisation*. Edited by H. Vollmer and D. Mills. Englewood Cliffs: Prentice-Hall.

Secord, P. F. and C. Backman. 1964. *Social Psychology*. New York: McGraw Hill, rev. edn, 1974.

Self, P. and H. J. Storing. 1962. *The State and the Farmer*. London: George Allen and Unwin.

Selznick, P. 1949. *TVA and the Grass Roots*. Berkeley: University of California Press.

Simon, H. A. 1953. Notes on the observation and measurement of power. *Journal of Politics*, 15.

Skocpol, T. 1979. *States and Social Revolutions*. Cambridge: Cambridge University Press.

Smelser, N. J. 1963. *Collective Behaviour*. London: Routledge and Kegan Paul.

Smith, M. J. 1990. *The Politics of Agricultural Support in Britain*. Aldershot: Dartmouth.

Smith, M. J. 1993. *Pressure, Power and Policy: State Autonomy and Policy Networks in Britain and the United States*. Hemel Hempstead: Harvester Wheatsheaf.

Soysal, Y. 1994. *Limits of Citizenship: Migrants and Postnational Membership in Europe*. Chicago: University of Chicago Press.

Stokman, F., R. Ziegler, and J. Scott (eds). 1985. *Networks of Corporate Power*. Cambridge: Polity.

Strange, S. 1988. *States and Markets*. London: Frances Pinter.

Sydie, R. A. 1987. *Natural Women, Cultured Men*. Buckingham: Open University Press.

Tarrow, S. 1994. *Power in Movement*. Cambridge: Cambridge University Press.

Thibaut, J. H. and H. H. Kelley. 1959. *The Social Psychology of Groups*. New York: John Wiley.

Thompson, J. B. 1995. *The Media and Modernity*. Cambridge: Polity.

Tilly, C. 1978. *From Mobilization to Revolution*. Reading: Addison Wesley.

Tilly, C. 1986. *The Contentious French*. Cambridge, Mass.: Harvard University Press.

Tilly, C. 1990. *Coercion, Capital, and European States*, AD *990–1990*. Oxford: Blackwell.

Tilly, C., L. Tilly, and R. Tilly. 1975. *The Rebellious Century, 1830–1930*. Cambridge, Mass.: Harvard University Press.

Truman, D. B. 1951. *The Governmental Process*. New York: Knopf.

Useem, M. 1984. *The Inner Circle*. New York: Oxford University Press.

Vogler, C. 1998. Money in the household: Some underlying issues of power. *Sociological Review*, 46.

Vogler, C. and J. Pahl. 1994. Money, power, and inequality within marriage. *Sociological Review*, 42.

Wallerstein, I. 1974. *The Modern World System I: Capitalist Agriculture and the Origins of the European World-economy in the Sixteenth Century*. New York: Academic Press.

Wallerstein, I. 1980. *The Modern World System II: Mercantilism and the Consolidation of the European World-economy, 1600–1750*. New York: Academic Press.

Wallerstein, I. 1989. *The Modern World System III: The Second Era of Great Expansion of the Capitalist World-economy, 1730–1840s*. New York: Academic Press.

Waltz, K. 1979. *Theory of International Politics*. Reading: Addison Wesley.

Warner, W. L. 1949. *Democracy in Jonesville*. New York: Harper and Brothers.

Wartenberg, T. 1990. *The Forms of Power: From Domination to Transformation*. Philadelphia: Temple University Press.

Weber, M. 1914. The economy and the arena of normative and de facto powers. In *Economy and Society*. Edited by G. Roth and C. Wittich. New York: Bedminster Press, 1968.

Weber, M. 1920. Conceptual Exposition. In *Economy and Society*. Edited by G. Roth and C. Wittich. New York: Bedminster Press, 1968.

Whitley, R., A. Thomas, and J. Marceau. 1981. *Masters of Business*. London: Tavistock.

Wilensky, H. 1967. *Organizational Intelligence*. New York: Basic Books.

Williamson, O. E. 1975. *Markets and Hierarchies*. New York: Free Press.

Wilson, G. 1977. *Special Interests and Policy Making*. London: John Wiley.

Witz, A. 1992. *Professions and Patriarchy*. London: Routledge.

Wolfe, D. M. 1959. Power and authority in the family. In *Studies in Social Power*. Edited by D. Cartwright. Ann Arbor: University of Michigan Press.

Wrong, D. 1961. The oversocialized concept of man in modern sociology. *American Sociological Review*, 26.

Wrong, D. 1967–8. Some problems in defining social power. In *Power*, vol. 1. Edited by J. Scott. London: Routledge, 1994.

Wrong, D. 1979. *Power: Its Forms, Bases, and Uses*. New Brunswick: Transaction Publishers, 1995.

Zeitlin, M. R. 1974. Corporate ownership and control: The large corporation and the capitalist class. In Zeitlin (1989).

Zeitlin, M. R. 1989. *The Large Corporation and the Capitalist Class*. Cambridge: Polity.

Zweigenhaft, R. and G. W. Domhoff. 1982. *Jews in the Protestant Establishment*. New York: Praeger.

Zweigenhaft, R. and G. W. Domhoff. 1991. *Blacks in the White Establishment? A Study of Race and Class in America*. New Haven: Yale University Press.

Index